LEGAL ISSUES
AND
RELIGIOUS COUNSELING

LEGAL ISSUES

AND

RELIGIOUS COUNSELING

RONALD K. BULLIS

CYNTHIA S. MAZUR

WESTMINSTER/JOHN KNOX PRESS
LOUISVILLE, KENTUCKY

Book design by Peggy Claire Calhoun

First edition

Published by Westminster/John Knox Press
Louisville, Kentucky

This book is printed on acid-free paper that meets the American National Standards Institute Z39.48 standard. ∞

PRINTED IN THE UNITED STATES OF AMERICA

9 8 7 6 5 4 3 2 1

Library of Congress Cataloging-in-Publication Data

Bullis, Ronald K.
    Legal issues and religious counseling / Ronald K. Bullis and
Cynthia S. Mazur. — 1st ed.
       p.   cm.
    Includes bibliographical references.
    ISBN 0-664-25386-5 (alk. paper)

    1. Pastoral counseling—Law and legislation—United States.
2. Clergy—Legal status, laws, etc.—United States.   3. Clergy—
Malpractice—United States.   Mazur, Cynthia S.
II. Title.
KF4868.C44B85   1993
346.7303'3—dc20   93-9379
[347.30633]

To my beloved parents, June and Chet Mazur,
And my dear grandmother, Lillian S. Bentham
—Cynthia S. Mazur

To Lori and Ray Bullis
Whose big hearts gave me body and soul
—Ronald K. Bullis

CONTENTS

Introduction   1

1. The First Amendment and Religious Counseling:
   A Legal Exegesis   7

2. Tort Law: Clergy Negligence, Clergy Malpractice,
   and the Duty to Protect the Counselee   22

3. The Expanding Vulnerability of Religious Counselors
   to Legal Action: Sexual Misconduct
   and the Duty to Protect Third Parties   33

4. State Regulation of Religious Counselors   44

5. Privileged Communication for Religious Counselors   68

6. Laws Limiting the Clergy Privilege   90

7. General Trends and Patterns
   of Religious Counseling Liability   102

8. A Legal Audit for Religious Counselors   111

   Glossary   121

   List of Abbreviations Used in References   125

INTRODUCTION

This volume describes, analyzes, and organizes the three types of legal issues most encountered by religious counselors. It is widely applicable to anyone working in religious institutions of any creed or denomination. Included are clergy, religious educators, church administrators, and church workers functioning in official capacities such as elders or deacons. The term "religious counseling" is broadly used here because religious counseling takes place in a variety of situations in religious organizations. Religious counseling can occur in almost every function of a religious organization—and so can lawsuits. Parish pastors and other religious professionals who offer counseling are open and vulnerable to lawsuits just as much as are those counselors who have a state license or certification.

For reasons explained herein, religious counselors are more vulnerable than ever to criminal prosecution and civil liability for acts arising out of their counseling or pastoral care activities. There are three particular categories of behavior for which religious counselors are being sued. These categories demand specific attention: (1) religious counselors are sued because the quality of the content of their religious counseling is alleged to be deficient; (2) religious counselors are sued because they reveal a confidence or privileged communication or fail to disclose such information when they are required to do so by law; and (3) religious counselors are sued based on allegations of sexual misconduct.

Because this book draws together aspects of religious counseling *and* law, this introduction will address issues of law for persons who have limited formal exposure to the principles and practice of American jurisprudence. "Getting shot at the border" is a wry comment made by many professionals crossing disciplinary lines. It means that professionals are safest within the confines of their own disciplines. Obviously, this book "crosses the border" between law and the practice of religious counseling. What follows, therefore, are several important points about the nature of law as it applies to religious counseling in an effort to assist the religious counselor effectively to cross the border.

The first point, and perhaps the most important point, is that state and federal law increasingly impact religious counselors and other religious professionals. If there were a time when religious institutions and religious professionals could work in blissful ignorance of or indifference to statutes, regulation, and cases—those days are gone. The reasons are twofold. First, the United States has become a litigious society, and, second, religious institutions no longer have the "charitable immunity" once afforded to them. Therefore, religious organizations, clergy, and other workers are increasingly amenable to suit and are increasingly held accountable for their actions or for their failure to act. In other words, religious counselors are increasingly likely to be sued, and Americans are increasingly availing themselves of the opportunity to bring such suits. Religious counselors are just as likely as psychiatrists, psychologists, or licensed counselors to be sued for events arising in the course of their counseling activities.

The second point is that the legal issues raised in this book apply to *all* clergy who conduct *any* type of counseling, including premarital, marriage, family, grief, or individual counseling. A religious professional devotes much time to counseling in hospitals or nursing homes, discussing premarital issues with couples planning to marry, preparing young people for confirmation, accompanying youth on trips or retreats, counseling individuals with religious, moral, or ethical problems, preparing individuals or couples for membership, or comforting persons confronting a death, divorce, or other loss in their life. All of these activities are counseling occasions—and also occasions for lawsuits. Thus, this book also directly applies to the activities of chaplains, religious educators, youth leaders, and anyone else working in a religious setting.

The applicability of this book to counselors working in pastoral counseling centers requires fuller discussion. As a general rule, the laws governing counseling discussed here apply to counselors in pastoral or religiously affiliated counseling centers as well.

Indeed, the three areas of conduct giving rise to suits are equally and fully applicable to pastoral counselors. Pastoral counselors must be concerned about their vulnerability to suit, particularly regarding sexual contact with clients, the laws regarding confidentiality, and the quality and content of their counseling. These three areas are primary examples of how the law both similarly and dissimilarly treats clergy and pastoral counselors.

2

Clergy enjoy broad rights under state privileged communication statutes, that is, the privilege to remain silent regarding information they know as a result of counseling despite the state's need for the information. California grants this privilege to clergy and their penitents. Pastoral counselors in California conducting marriage counseling do not enjoy this privilege, however, even though California grants a confidentiality privilege to psychotherapists and their patients.

In approximately half of the criminal statutes prohibiting counselor sexual misconduct with counselees, clergy are specifically designated. All of these statutes, however, prohibit sexual misconduct by psychotherapists or those who purport to conduct psychotherapy.

The requirements regarding the quality and content of counseling can be different for pastoral counselors and clergy. Again using California as an example, nontherapist counselors are held to a lower standard than are psychiatrists and licensed psychotherapists. The nontherapist counselor is under no legal obligation to refer a suicidal counselee to a counselor trained in assisting the suicidal person. If, however, the nontherapist holds herself out as a professional, she could be held liable for injuries related to her counseling activities. Thus, regarding the three areas where religious counselors are most susceptible to suit, licensed pastoral counselors need to be just as well acquainted with the issues and potential pitfalls.

Clergy designated as "pastoral counselors" by either state certification, licensure, or registration, or by virtue of membership in the American Association of Pastoral Counselors or the Association for Clinical Pastoral Education, are governed by the ordinances of their respective associations and by applicable state law. Such clergy and other counselors need to examine their specific state law and association regulations for certification, advertising, and other duties.

Payment for counseling services is not, in and of itself, a determining factor for liability. Even if a counselor takes no payment for counseling services, the counselor is held to the same legal standard of conduct imposed for all counselors. Similarly, clergy are vulnerable to suits even though they do not generally charge separately for their services.

Third, the issues raised in this book apply across denominational lines. The term "clergy" as defined in state statutes and by state courts has broad denotations. The cases included in this volume are current illustrations of some of these legal definitions and suggest that no denomination has a monopoly on litigation.

Fourth, this is a handbook, not a cookbook. Cookbooks give precise recipes to attain precise results. The American legal system pays scrupulous attention to procedural detail. Only attorneys are capable of sorting out the specific facts of a situation and applying the appropriate law. No book is capable of determining the legal outcome of a specific fact pattern. Therefore, this book does not intend to replace legal counsel. Readers should direct specific questions to lawyers competent in legal issues pertaining to both religion and counseling.

Handbooks, on the other hand, raise issues in a comprehensive manner broadly applicable to the field. This handbook provides an overview of legal issues and legal precedent with charts and a glossary. This book is valuable for all religious counselors and religious professionals because it can help prevent possible lawsuits and other legal entanglements. Knowing the potential dangers can raise "red flags" of caution and prudence among religious counselors. Conversely, knowledge can also be a wonderful source of freedom from the exaggerated fears surrounding much uninformed discussions of religion, counseling, and the law.

Additionally, this book can help religious counselors take a more active role in their own litigation. Lawyers can only accomplish their best with the fullest, most informed help from their clients. When a religious counselor knows the pertinent facts and best evidence to place in his or her lawyer's hand, much time, money, energy, and even reputation can be spared.

To conclude, a series of suggestions on how to understand and interpret the relevance of statutes and case law may be helpful. Laws passed by state or federal legislatures are compiled into statutory or regulatory codes. Courts apply statutes and other court decisions (i.e., case law) to specific fact patterns. For example, a state privileged communication law may designate "clergy" as those who enjoy the privilege. However, whether or not a current Presbyterian elder or a Roman Catholic nun is considered "clergy" for the purposes of privileged communication law may have to be decided by the courts in interpreting the statute.

1. Case law interprets statutory law. It is not for judges to create law; this function is reserved for state or federal legislators. However, the line between *interpreting* law and *creating* law is a fine and blurry one. A famous example is *Brown v. Topeka Board of Education,* where the U.S. Supreme Court prohibited segregated schools. The Constitution prohibited discrimination, but the Court had to interpret whether that prohibition, in effect, required integration.

2. Law is extremely hierarchical. Each state and the federal government have a hierarchical court system. The "trial" courts have less power and are superseded by "higher" courts of appeal. Thus, a defendant can appeal his or her case from the lower and intermediate courts to the highest state court, and, in rare cases, may even appeal the case to the U.S. Supreme Court.

The authors have been careful to designate whether an illustrative case is at the trial or appellate level. A trial court decision can be over-ruled, reversed, or otherwise modified by an appellate court. Decisions at the trial court level have authority for other trial courts in that state.

The names for the state hierarchy of courts might be confusing. Three examples of court systems are listed below, from lowest to highest.

	New York	Virginia	Federal
(lowest)	Supreme Court	District Court	District Court
	Supreme Court, Appellate Division	Circuit Court	Circuit Court
(highest)	Court of Appeals	Court of Appeals	Supreme Court
		Supreme Court	

3. Statutes can be changed and cases can be modified. Legislators have been known, from time to time, to repeal, to change, and even to create seemingly contradictory laws. It is for the courts to sort out contradictions and to determine the intent of statutes in light of specific fact patterns.

4. Case law is based upon precedent. Judges are not lone rangers and do not interpret law in a legal vacuum. They are bound to interpret law in light of previous decisions—the doctrine of *stare decisis*. Precedent guides subsequent decisions. Thus, court opinions which are based upon prior decisions, in turn guide future judicial action. The decisions described and explained in this volume should be examined both for what they immediately decide and for how they may influence future decisions.

Furthermore, state court decisions in one state are *not* precedent in another state. Each state court may interpret its own state law according to its own court's prior decisions. Even a decision from one state's highest court cannot determine the decision of the lowest court from another state. However, in the area of suits against religious counselors, an area without much prior history, the courts will be influenced by the cases of other states. Lawyers, also, will point the court to well-reasoned opinions or similar fact patterns of cases from other states.

5. Case law is highly fact-driven. Although statutory law is written in broad legislative strokes, case law uses a finer brush. It must examine the legally relevant facts surrounding each dispute, apply the appropriate law, and render a cognizable decision. Facts are extremely important in rendering a fair and sound decision. Readers are encouraged to scrutinize closely the facts of the illustrative cases noted in this book. Even slight differences in facts can change the outcome of cases.

6. The law is fraught with ambiguities. Jury decisions and judicial decisions are based on numerous subjective factors. For example, witnesses are judged for credibility and personal nuances that go far beyond the written transcripts of testimony. Different attorneys, different jurors, and different states can and do construe similar fact patterns in very different ways. The outcome of the Rodney King criminal trial exemplifies the subjective interpretations that are possible even when the evidence seems immutable, as in that case where the evidence was memorialized on videotape.

The issues and themes discussed in this book illustrate the law as it is currently and suggest likely trends. Although legal issues and trends will undoubtedly change through the coming years, the reader will acquire a sound basis for understanding the law and preventing infractions and liability. Thus, this book is broadly applicable to religious counselors, clergy, pastoral counselors, and all those who work in religious organizations.

1

THE FIRST AMENDMENT
AND RELIGIOUS COUNSELING:
A LEGAL EXEGESIS

*I can't be a clergyman, I haven't got convictions. And then, I can't
pronounce the names right in the Bible. They are very difficult, in the
Old Testament particularly.*

—Henry James, Portrait of a Lady

Introduction

Religious counselors are being sued for predominantly three types of
conduct: (1) the religious counselor may be sued if a counselee attempts
suicide or attempts to hurt a third party; the nature of the advice given
by the religious counselor and the responsibility of the counselor to protect the counselee or the third party is called into question (Taylor, 1990);
(2) the religious counselor may be sued because he/she is accused of
sexual contact with a counselee; and (3) the religious counselor may be
sued because he/she breached a confidence; that is, he/she made private counseling information public or failed to breach a confidence
when doing so is required by law or could prevent harm to an innocent
third party (e.g., suspected child abuse). How a particular court views
the role of the Constitution will influence whether the court will find the
clergy liable or not.

Although religious counselors are familiar with the U.S. Constitution and the American legal system in general, many are less familiar
with the complex relationship among the courts, the Constitution, religious freedom, and the standards for religious conduct. A brief
overview of this relationship is presented in this chapter to provide a
basic foundation by which the reader can better understand the lawsuits, brought both by and against religious counselors, that are discussed in the rest of this volume. Every court reviewing religious
counseling will begin by determining the relationship of the First
Amendment to the facts of the case. The religion clauses of the U.S. Constitution play heavily into the wide range of legal opinions reviewing
clergy behavior.

7

The U.S. Constitution

Religious convictions, as well as freedom from religious indoctrination, are protected pursuant to the laws of the United States. Religious freedoms flow from the U.S. Constitution and from some federal and state statutes. The First Amendment of the Constitution embodies two religious rights. The first is the "free exercise clause," and the second is the "freedom from establishment clause."

Byron White, a former Episcopalian Justice of the Supreme Court, appointed by President Kennedy in 1962 and famous for being the National Football League's highest paid player while attending law school at Yale, states that "most of the constitutional law is not to be found by reading the Constitution, which is a very short document." (*Third Branch*, 1986). The two religion clauses of the First Amendment as set forth in the Bill of Rights read:

> Congress shall make no law respecting an establishment of religion, or prohibiting the free exercise thereof . . .

Additionally, the right not to be discriminated against on the basis of religion is embodied in the Fourteenth Amendment:

> nor shall any State . . . deny to any person within its jurisdiction the equal protection of the laws.

Before the Fourteenth Amendment was passed, some states persisted in discriminating against particular religions. In North Carolina, officeholders were required to believe in the Protestant religion. Maryland limited civil office to Christians and allowed taxation to support the Christian religion. The Constitution was initially written to limit the power of the federal government. Later, these limitations were also placed on the state's authority over its respective citizens.

The right not to be discriminated against on the basis of religion is found also in various federal statutes, for example, the Civil Rights Act of 1964 (employer may not discriminate against employees or prospective employees on the basis of race, color, religion, sex, or national origin), among others. Additionally, religious rights may be protected by state law. For instance, recently a California court struck down the use of a preemployment psychiatric test for security guards that inquired into their religious beliefs. (*Soroka v. Dayton Hudson Corp.*, 1991). In order to determine their fitness for employment, applicants were asked whether they believed in an afterlife or the second coming of Christ.

The freedom to follow one's religious beliefs and the freedom to be free from the state's enforced religion have resulted in a doctrine of religious immunity that pastors may raise in their defense if they get sued.

Religious, or First Amendment, immunity may shield the pastor from suit because the court has no authority to regulate religious matters.

The Free Exercise Clause

In 1940, the Supreme Court determined for the first time that government action impermissibly interfered with an individual's free exercise rights, in a case involving the conviction of several Jehovah's Witnesses for breach of the peace. (*Cantwell v. Connecticut*, 1940). The family of Jehovah's Witnesses was going from home to home in a Roman Catholic neighborhood with a portable phonograph and a record, which the family asked each resident if it could play. The record promoted the sale of Jehovah's Witness literature and also included an attack on the Roman Catholic religion. The Court examined the free exercise clause:

> Freedom of conscience and freedom to adhere to such religious organization or form of worship as the individual may choose cannot be restricted by law. On the other hand, it safeguards the free exercise of the chosen form of religion. Thus the Amendment embraces two concepts, freedom to believe and freedom to act. The first is absolute but, in the nature of things, the second cannot be. Conduct remains subject to regulation for the protection of society.

The Court reversed the convictions.

Four years later, the Supreme Court in *United States v. Ballard* again examined the free exercise clause. In *Ballard*, a family was convicted for using the mail to defraud the public in promoting the "I am" movement. The family alleged that it had abilities to heal and cure infirmities. The Court reversed the convictions, finding that the lower court must withhold from the jury all questions concerning the truth or falsity of the religious beliefs or doctrines of the Ballards. Writing for the Court, Justice Douglas stated:

> Freedom of thought, which includes freedom of religious belief, is basic in a society of free men. It embraces the right to maintain theories of life and of death and of the hereafter which are rank heresy to followers of the orthodox faiths. Heresy trials are foreign to our Constitution. Men may believe what they cannot prove. They may not be put to the proof of their religious doctrines or beliefs. Religious experiences which are as real as life to some may be incomprehensible to others. Yet the fact that they may be beyond the ken of mortals does not mean that they can be made suspect before the law. Many take their gospel from the New Testament. But it would hardly be supposed that they could be tried before a jury charged with the duty of determining whether those teachings contained false representations. The miracles

of the New Testament, the Divinity of Christ, life after death, the power of prayer are deep in the religious convictions of many. If one could be sent to jail because a jury in a hostile environment found those teachings false, little indeed would be left of religious freedom. (Citations omitted.)

Until recently, infringement of religious freedom was gauged by a two-part test, questioning whether the government action or law imposed a substantial burden on the free exercise of religion, and if so, whether it was justified by a compelling state interest. The test was set forth in the 1963 case of *Sherbert v. Verner*, the first case to create a religious exemption.

In *Sherbert*, a Seventh Day Adventist was discharged because she would not work on Saturdays. She was unable to find other employment because of her refusal to work on Saturdays and, of necessity, filed a claim for unemployment benefits. The South Carolina Commission denied Sherbert's application because she would not accept suitable work when offered, although these offers required work on Saturdays. The Supreme Court found no compelling state interest that would justify the substantial infringement on the employee's right to religious freedom. The Supreme Court created a religious exemption from the eligibility provisions of unemployment compensation laws because these provisions unfairly burdened Sherbert's free exercise rights.

Pastors Enjoy a Free Exercise Right to Counsel Without Conforming to State Licensure Laws

Although most states have statutes requiring that counselors be licensed and formally qualified, licensure for pastors whose duties include counseling, traditionally, has not been required. Thus, clergy have been allowed a specific exemption from certain levels of education and skill required of secular counselors. This religious exemption has its genesis in the free exercise clause and has created an autonomous area for clergy that courts and legislators are reluctant to regulate.

In *State v. Motherwell* (1990), Washington State enacted a mandatory reporting statute for specifically designated professionals, not including clergy, who learned of child abuse. Three religious counselors (only one of whom was ordained at the time of the offense) faced criminal prosecution for failing to report, within forty-eight hours pursuant to the statute, child abuse disclosed during counseling. The three allegations included a woman stating that her husband had sexually abused her daughter, a woman stating that her husband had beaten their two young sons, and a woman stating that her husband was sexually abusing their eight-year-old daughter. All three counselors received a deferred sentence, probation, compulsory professional education, and one received a $500 fine. All three appealed.

Although admitting that their religion did not require them to keep confidential all information learned in a counseling session, the counselors argued that their rights to exercise their religion freely would be denied by the imposition of the statute. As religious counselors, their practice was to tend to their parishioners' problems through prayer and counseling and to inform the secular authorities only in those cases where their religious procedures proved ineffective.

A special panel made up of all of Washington's Supreme Court judges heard the argument presented by the counselors' attorney as follows:

> [The church counselors] sincerely believe that as ministers . . . they are "called" to serve . . . their congregation. Their spiritual counseling and care are based on the Bible, require prayer, and focus on a parishioner's problems in a private setting with the goals of repentance, healing and reconciliation.
>
> Imposition of mandatory 48-hour reporting would undermine the trust between minister and present and future counselees. . . . Under the statute as applied to defendants and other clergy, the minister is no longer a confidant, but a witness for the State; not an instrument of spiritual guidance, but a conscripted arm of the police.

The ordained minister convinced the court that ordained ministers were not compelled to report because clergy were not specifically mentioned in the statute. Thus, his conviction was reversed. The other two religious counselors, however, were subject to the statute because they met the statutory definition of social workers. Moreover, in response to a First Amendment protection argument, the court reasoned that mandatory reporting did not prevent these two religious counselors from counseling their parishioners in accordance with their faith. Its decision might have been different, the court stated, if the mandatory reporting laws coerced a direct violation of the counselors' religious tenets. Finding a compelling state interest, the court held that "the State's interest in the protection of children is unquestionably of the utmost importance."

The Uncertain Future of the Free Exercise Clause

The Compelling State Interest Test Is Abandoned

The free exercise clause, solidly embedded as it is in the Constitution, cannot be abrogated unless there is a constitutional amendment. The Supreme Court, however, can reevaluate its interpretation of the free exercise clause and apply it differently to different sets of facts. For instance, in

1878, the Court determined that Mormons do not have a free exercise right to practice polygamy, which violated federal crimina! law. (*Reynolds v. United States*, 1879). In 1972, the Supreme Court determined that Amish parents have a free exercise right to violate a state criminal law involving compulsory education of their children. (*Wisconsin v. Yoder*, 1972). Using the compelling state interest test of *Sherbert v. Verner*, the Court found that Wisconsin had failed to show that its interest in educating its citizens outweighed or would be adversely affected by granting a religious exemption to the Amish.

In 1990, the Supreme Court dismantled the compelling state interest test to the horror of many churches and the astonishment of many constitutional scholars. In *Employment Div., Dep't of Human Resources v. Smith*, two drug and alcohol rehabilitation counselors were fired for ingesting peyote pursuant to the religious practices of the Native American Church. Both counselors applied for and were denied unemployment compensation. The counselors argued that they had not been fired for good cause and should not be denied compensation.

Justice Scalia wrote the Court opinion, finding that the free exercise clause cannot be used to authorize religious conduct that conflicts with a generally applicable, religion-neutral state regulation. Scalia virtually abandoned the compelling state interest test and stated that in the past the free exercise claims had only prevailed when they had been coupled with other constitutional rights such as free speech. (See *Cantwell* above.) Indeed, Scalia stated that the compelling state interest test allowed a person, by virtue of his/her beliefs, to become a law unto him/herself.

Although some scholars believe that Scalia's new test is applicable only to state criminal laws, others point out that it is these criminal laws that place the greatest burden on the free exercise rights and from which religious practices deserve the greatest degree of constitutional protection. (Choper, 1990). Less popular religions would not fare as well under his new test, admitted Scalia, as they had under the compelling state interest test.

The *Smith* decision has had a significant impact on the religious community as courts all over the country have tried to decipher what it means. In New York City, St. Bartholomew's Church argued that it should be exempt from a landmark preservation ordinance that prevented it from altering and adding a high rise to its building. One hundred and fifty million dollars for church mission work was at stake. Applying *Smith*, the federal appellate court determined that the church was bound by the ordinance. In other states, both Jews and Vietnamese have asserted a religious right to prevent the autopsy of a loved one. In view of *Smith*, the courts are disregarding these claims. The Occupational Safety and Health Administration (OSHA) for fifteen years granted a religious exemption from the wearing of hard hats to those who wear a turban for religious purposes. It withdrew this exemption after *Smith* was decided. Zoning ordinances excluding churches from commercial districts have been upheld, and churches have been required to participate in workers' compensation plans. The courts' interpretation of *Smith* continues to curtail rights that churches previously took for granted, for it is believed that religious exemptions from generally applicable, religion-neutral laws have been eviscerated by the decision.

Congress Reacts

In the summer of 1990, Congressman Stephen Solarz (D/NY) introduced the Religious Freedom Restoration Act, which states in part:

> The purposes of this Act [are]
> (1) to restore the compelling interest test as set forth in Sherbert v. Verner and Wisconsin v. Yoder and to guarantee its application in all cases where free exercise of religion is burdened; and
> (2) to provide a claim or defense to persons whose religious exercise is burdened by government.
>
> . . . .
>
> Government may burden a person's exercise of religion only if it demonstrates that application of the burden to the person
> (1) is essential to further a compelling governmental interest; and
> (2) is the least restrictive means of furthering that compelling governmental interest.

At the time of this writing, passage of the bill seems likely, although its initial, overwhelming support has waned due to concerns raised by the United States Catholic Conference. In the fall of 1990, the Catholic Conference stated that religious liberty arguments supporting the right to choose an abortion must be specifically excluded from the protections of the bill.

If the act is passed and becomes law, this law would not change the Constitution and would not change the Supreme Court's interpretation of the free exercise clause. Authority to uphold religious freedom pursuant to the new act would flow from the supremacy clause of the Fourteenth Amendment.

The Supreme Court Is Not Finished

An additional twist to the free exercise saga involves the fact that in March of 1992 the Supreme Court agreed to decide another free exercise case. (*Church of the Lukumi Babalu Aye v. City of Hialeah*, 1992). Hialeah, a city in Florida, has denied the right to practice animal sacrifice to adherents of Santeria, an ancient African religion practiced in the Caribbean and brought to the United States by Cubans. Hialeah banned animal sacrifice in religious ceremonies but allows the killing of animals for other purposes. For instance, the state allows hunting, fishing, and trapping, animal shelters to kill animals, animals to be fed to other animals, and the killing of animals for research. The city asserts, as the basis for its ordinance, that it must regulate the health of the community, protect animals, and safeguard the psychological well-being of children.

The Supreme Court has always maintained that religious conduct posing a substantial threat to public safety, peace, or order may be regulated. In *Jacobson v. Massachusetts* (1905), the Supreme Court upheld compulsory vaccination despite parental religious objections; in *Prince v. Massachusetts* (1944), child labor laws were upheld despite religiously motivated work by children in preaching and selling religious tracts on the street.

The *Lukumi* case is similar to *Smith* in that the banning of a central, religious ritual is at issue. The Hialeah ordinance is different, however, in that it specifically bans a particular religious practice of an individual church while allowing the same conduct for secular purposes. One of the rationales in *Smith* had been that Oregon's law prohibiting drug use was applicable to everyone, a religious-neutral law of general applicability. *Lukumi* was argued before the High Court in November of 1992 and will be decided sometime before July of 1993.

The Establishment Clause

The *Lemon* Test

The establishment clause requires government neutrality toward religion in order to maintain the integrity of each institution. The government is forbidden from passing a law or engaging in any conduct, such as placing religious symbols on the town square, that establishes or promotes religion. The controlling standard in the establishment clause arena is commonly called the *Lemon* test. (*Lemon v. Kurtzman*, 1971).

To pass constitutional muster pursuant to the *Lemon* test, the statute or government action under review must (1) have a secular purpose; (2) not have as its primary effect the advancing or inhibiting of religion; and (3) not result in excessive entanglement between government and religion. Regarding a law authorizing prayer in school classrooms in Alabama, the Court found that the law had a religious purpose. (*Wallace v. Jaffree*, 1985). The sponsor of the law had inserted into the legislative record that the purpose of the law was to return prayer to the public schools. Justice O'Connor indicated that had the law simply authorized a moment of silence and had the record evidenced a secular purpose, the law may have passed the *Lemon* test. Each of the three prongs of the test must be satisfied before the law or conduct will be upheld as constitutional.

Examining a city-erected nativity scene set among other holiday displays in Rhode Island, the Court stated that the city had a secular purpose for including the nativity scene in the Christmas display. (*Lynch v. Donnelly*, 1984). This purpose, found the Court, was merely to depict the origins of the holiday.

The first prong of the *Lemon* test, which focuses on the purpose of the government action or the statute, has resulted in a spate of inconsistent results. Indeed, in a case that seems to stand alone, the Court determined that daily prayers opening state legislative sessions were valid because they were the result of two centuries of history. (*Marsh v. Chambers*, 1983). Clearly, these prayers do not have a secular purpose.

The *Lemon* test has been applied in a wide variety of situations. Some of the cases review direct or indirect aid to religious schools or challenges to religious conduct in public schools. These cases often examine whether aid, books, tutoring, transportation, and so forth, will have as its primary effect the advancement of religion or whether monitoring such aid will involve the government in excessive entanglement. In this area, the Court affords the greatest protection from government establishment of religion to elementary and secondary school children.

The Future of the *Lemon* Test

Recently, the Supreme Court has begun to turn away from the *Lemon* test. Scholars have suggested that a new test is evolving. (Choper, 1989). The problem is obtaining agreement on a proper replacement. One new test set forth by Justice O'Connor and agreed with by Justices Blackmun and Stevens simply asks "whether a reasonable observer would perceive the government action as endorsement of religion." (*Id.*) Such a test greatly increases the government's ability to act in ways or to pass statutes that have religious elements. In addition, Justices Kennedy, White, Rehnquist, and Scalia have advanced an even less restrictive test, stating that "there must be coercion: either direct compulsion or significant expenditure of tax funds, or something amounting to proselytization on the part of the state." (*Id.*)

In June of 1992, the Supreme Court decided *Lee v. Weisman. Weisman* involves a parent who became upset while attending his daughter's eighth-grade graduation, which began with an invocation and ended with a benediction. Weisman is Jewish, and the religious leader officiating was a rabbi. The Bush administration asked the Court to replace the *Lemon* test with the question of "whether the practice at issue provides direct benefits to a religion in a manner that threatens the establishment of an official church or compels persons to participate in a religion or religious activity contrary to their consciences." (U.P.I., 1991).

The Court declined to reconsider, relax, or even apply the standards of the *Lemon* test because it found that the state action so clearly violated the establishment clause. The Court determined that these prayers created a state-sponsored and state-directed religious exercise in a public school. The government may not coerce anyone to support or participate in a religious exercise. The question as to the future of the *Lemon* test was left open.

When Government Action Favors One Specific Religion

The establishment clause also prohibits the state and federal government from passing laws that prefer one religion over another. (*Everson v. Board of Educ.*, 1947). In *Larson v. Valente* (1982), religious denominations under Minnesota law receiving more than 50 percent of their funds from members and affiliated organizations were not required to comply with registration and reporting laws regarding their fund-raising activities. This statute had the effect of granting a denominational preference to well-established churches. When one church is favored over another, the *Lemon* test is dispensed with, and the much stricter compelling state interest test set forth in *Larson* is applied.

Pursuant to this test as stated in *Larson:* (1) the state must have a compelling interest that supports its action; and (2) the state must have a well-thought-out explanation as to how its action is closely fitted to furthering its compelling state interest. Although the Supreme Court agreed that Minnesota had a compelling state interest in protecting its citizens from abusive solicitation practices, it found that Minnesota had not demonstrated that its exemption was necessary to further that interest nor that the exemption was closely fitted to furthering the interest. Finding that the statutory exemption failed to pass its strict analysis, the Supreme Court extended the exemption to the Unification Church of Sun Myung Moon, holding that any bona fide religion would qualify for the registration and reporting exemption.

When Government Action Favors Religion in General

There is serious debate among church/state scholars as to how much government accommodation of religion was intended by the framers and early interpreters of the Constitution. (Curry, 1987, 204–209). The government accommodates religion, for example, when it grants a religious tax exemption. In *Walz v. Tax Commission* (1970), a property owner in New York State sought to eradicate tax exemptions for religious organizations by arguing that religious exemptions impermissibly establish religion in violation of the First Amendment. The Supreme Court stated that the exemption did not establish, sponsor, or support religion; it simply spared churches from the burden of property taxation levied on profit organizations. Indeed, the Court determined that a religious property tax exemption would guarantee the free exercise of all forms of religious belief.

The difficulty in complying with the establishment clause while accommodating religion is readily apparent. For instance, notwithstanding *Walz*, the Supreme Court recently struck down a Texas sales tax that exempted religious publications. Publishers of secular magazines had argued that the exemption favored religion in violation of the establishment clause. The Court agreed. (*Texas Monthly, Inc. v. Bullock*, 1989).

Many individuals and organizations have brought suits in the lower courts to stop the government from granting a preferential position to religion. Madalyn Murray O'Hair has challenged state laws that require that a person believe in a supreme being before he/she may hold public office or serve on a jury. Among other things, she has challenged the papal Mass on the National Mall, to no avail.

In an unusual case, upon which the movie *Footloose* was based, a local school board's rule prohibiting dances on school property was challenged by some of the high school students. The students argued that the ban was in essence an establishment of religion on school grounds because it was based on local religious tenets condemning dancing as sinful. The court ruled that the board's decision did not violate the establishment clause, finding that dancing is a wholly secular activity with absolutely no religious component. Thus, the rule had a secular purpose and did not advance religion.

As mentioned above, similarly situated groups are using the establishment clause to challenge laws that give religious groups an unfair advantage over their secular counterparts. For example, secular day-care centers brought an action in Virginia because the state allows religious day-care centers to be exempt from licensing requirements. (*Forest Hills Early Learning Center, Inc. v. Grace Baptist Church*, 1988). These requirements relate to space, health, nutrition, disciplinary practices, and parental participation. The court stated that a statute exempting church-run day-care centers from licensing requirements was simply adopting a hands-off policy. The government could not be accused of advancing religion. Moreover, the exemption lessened the risk of entanglement, the court asserted, because the state would not be overseeing the church's compliance.

The Establishment Clause and Chaplains

Taxpayers have challenged the public funding of chaplains as a violation of the establishment clause. The payment of chaplains in the Senate and

House has been upheld based upon two centuries of history. The payment of chaplains in the military has been upheld because the service members have free exercise rights that must be preserved.

In one recent case, taxpayers brought a suit in Iowa to challenge a county hospital's hiring of a chaplain. (*Carter v. Broadlawns Medical Center*, 1988). Broadlawns Medical Center served the county's indigent. Fifty percent of the patients were residents of the psychiatric ward, with one third of these being committed involuntarily. The rest of the patients were in a chemical abuse unit or were prisoners who needed treatment.

The chaplain's job description called for consistent pastoral care throughout the hospital, adding spiritual support and counseling to the ongoing healing effort. It was the hospital's position that in situations of grave illness, insanity, and death, religious problems exist that must be dealt with no matter how secular the hospital.

The court upheld the county's right to fund the chaplain's salary for two reasons. First, most of the patients were not free to leave, and their free exercise rights had to be preserved. Thus, funding the chaplain's salary would be a permissible accommodation of the patients' free exercise rights. In addition, the court found that the chaplaincy had a secular purpose of helping the patients get well with a "holistic" treatment approach.

In a slightly different situation, a county social worker was fired for administering spiritual counseling and treatment to incarcerated men. (*Spratt v. County of Kent*, 1985). The social worker read the Bible, prayed, addressed spiritual issues, and cast out demons. He insisted that it would have been a violation of his religious beliefs to refuse to offer religious counseling to the inmates. The court upheld the termination, nonetheless, stating that as a county employee, the social worker had to maintain government's religious neutrality.

The Nexus Between the Two Religion Clauses

Each religion clause carried to an extreme violates the other. If the government supported the free exercise of religion to extreme, it would be violating its duty to refrain from establishing religion. If the government separated church and state too forcibly, the free exercise rights of the people would be infringed.

One of the great, modern constitutional scholars, Harvard Law Professor Laurence Tribe, has stated that where the two religion clauses are in conflict, the free exercise clause should be dominant. "Such dominance is the natural result of tolerating religion as broadly as possible rather than thwarting at all costs even the faintest appearance of establishment." (Tribe, 1988, 1201).

Although at first glance the free exercise clause and the freedom from establishment clause appear very different, they can quickly become difficult to separate. For instance, in 1989 the lawyer for Jimmy Swaggart Ministries (JSM), a nonprofit religious organization that conducted crusades and sold religious materials, argued against the imposition of a sales and use tax. JSM asserted to the Supreme Court that these taxes would place a significant burden on the organization's right to exercise freely its practices and beliefs. (*Jimmy Swaggart Ministries v. Board of Equalization*, 1990). JSM also argued, however, that administering a tax on the organization would involve the government in "excessive entanglement" between the government and religion, a result that is prohibited by the establishment clause. The Court decided that the payment of taxes does not significantly burden the organization's religious practices or beliefs under the free exercise clause. Additionally, the Court found that the government's collection of the tax did not create an excessive entanglement between the government and religion because it involved no inquiry into religious doctrine or close scrutiny of activities.

The interrelated nature of the two clauses is similarly exemplified in the interesting case wherein people brought suit to enjoin the distribution of the film *The Last Temptation of Christ*. The plaintiffs alleged that the film infringed their freedom of worship by portraying Christ in a defamatory manner. The court stated that to decide the "correct" interpretation of the life of Christ would violate the establishment clause, for the court would be required to make inquiry into religious doctrine to establish the correct interpretation of the Christian faith. (*Nayak v. MCA, Inc.*, 1990).

Finally, a Kansas court recently required a defendant to attend a specific church as a condition of his probation. Such government action helps to establish religion in general, in addition to endorsing a specific church. The court action was struck down by an appeals court as a violation of the free exercise clause, which prohibits forced religious indoctrination. (*Kansas v. Evans*, 1990).

State Law

Most states have enacted state constitutions that are similar to the federal Constitution. Some of these afford fewer religious freedoms than does the U.S. Constitution. For example, before the Supreme Court decided the *Smith* case, Oregon's highest court had determined that although the actions of the two drug counselors were not protected by Oregon's rights of religious freedom, their actions were protected under the free exercise clause of the U.S. Constitution. Regarding its exclusive province, that is, the interpretation of the U.S. Constitution, the Supreme Court disagreed.

A state constitution may grant its residents greater religious protections than does the U.S. Constitution. In the aftermath of the *Smith* decision, a Minnesota court stated that although the state requirement that the Amish display an orange fluorescent triangle on their buggies did not violate the U.S. Constitution, such a requirement did violate the state right to religious freedom. An Amish man had brought the suit, asking if he could use reflective tape and a lantern instead of the offensive modern triangle. (*Minnesota v. Hershberger*, 1990).

Religious rights in America are a multifaceted array of ever changing laws and court cases. Many scholars believe that the religion clauses will be developed in the coming decade more than at any other time in history. Ground-breaking decisions shedding light on whole new areas of religious rights will be written over the next couple of years. Thus, it remains to be seen whether free exercise rights will be restricted and whether freedom from establishment rights will be expanded.

References

Cantwell v. Connecticut, 310 U.S. 296 (1940).

Carter v. Broadlawns Medical Center, 857 F.2d 448 (8th Cir. 1988), *cert. denied*, 489 U.S. 1096 (1989).

Choper, J. H. 59 U.S.L.W. 2275 (U.S. Nov. 6, 1990).

———. 58 U.S.L.W. 2204 (U.S. Oct. 10, 1989).

Church of the Lukumi Babalu Aye v. City of Hialeah, 112 S. Ct. 1472 (1992).

Curry, T. J. (1987). *First Freedoms: Church and State in America to the Passage of the First Amendment*. New York: Oxford University Press.

Employment Div., Dep't of Human Resources v. Smith, 494 U.S. 872 (1990).

Everson v. Board of Educ., 330 U.S. 1 (1947).

Forest Hills Early Learning Center, Inc. v. Grace Baptist Church, 846 F.2d 260 (4th Cir. 1988), *cert. denied*, 488 U.S. 1029 (1989).

Jacobson v. Massachusetts, 197 U.S. 11 (1905).

Jimmy Swaggart Ministries v. Board of Equalization, 493 U.S. 378 (1990).

Kansas v. Evans, 14 Kan. App. 2d 591, 796 P.2d 178 (1990).

Larson v. Valente, 456 U.S. 228 (1982).

Lee v. Weisman, 112 S. Ct. 2649 (1992).

Lemon v. Kurtzman, 403 U.S. 602 (1971).

Lynch v. Donnelly, 465 U.S. 668 (1984).

Marsh v. Chambers, 463 U.S. 783 (1983).

Minnesota v. Hershberger, 462 N.W.2d 393 (1990).

Nayak v. MCA, Inc., 911 F.2d 1082 (5th Cir. 1990), *cert. denied,* 111 S. Ct. 962 (1991).

Prince v. Massachusetts, 321 U.S. 158 (1944).

Reynolds v. United States, 98 U.S. 145 (1879).

Sherbert v. Verner, 374 U.S. 398 (1963).

Soroka v. Dayton Hudson Corp., 235 Cal. App. 3d 654, 1 Cal. Rptr. 2d 77 (1991), *review granted,* 4 Cal. Rptr. 2d 180, 822 P.2d 1327 (1992).

Spratt v. County of Kent, 621 F. Supp. 594 (W.D. Mich. 1985), *aff'd,* 810 F.2d 203 (1986), *cert. denied,* 480 U.S. 934 (1987).

State v. Motherwell, 114 Wash. 2d 353, 788 P.2d 1066 (1990).

Taylor, M. (1990). *Nally v. Grace Community Church:* The Future of Clergy Malpractice Under Content-Based Analysis. *Utah Law Review, 1990,* 661–683.

Texas Monthly, Inc. v. Bullock, 489 U.S. 1 (1989).

The Third Branch. (November, 1986). "Justices Discuss Constitution, Affirmative Action, Death Penalty, Bicentennial Celebration Plans at Circuit Judicial Conferences." *The Third Branch* 18, no. 11:2.

Tribe, L. H. (1988). *American Constitutional Law* (2d ed.). Mineola, N.Y.: Foundation Press.

United States v. Ballard, 322 U.S. 78 (1944).

U.P.I., Mar. 18, 1991 (QuikNews).

Wallace v. Jaffree, 472 U.S. 38 (1985).

Walz v. Tax Commission, 397 U.S. 664 (1970).

Wisconsin v. Yoder, 406 U.S. 205 (1972).

2
TORT LAW: CLERGY NEGLIGENCE, CLERGY MALPRACTICE, AND THE DUTY TO PROTECT THE COUNSELEE

Because it is requisite, that [none] should come to the holy Communion, but with a full trust in God's mercy, and with a quiet conscience; therefore if there be any of you, who by this means cannot quiet [their] own conscience herein, but requireth further comfort or counsel, let [them] come to me, or to some other discreet and learned Minister of God's Word, and open [their] grief.

—*1662 Prayer Book*

Negligence

Counselees are bringing tort suits against religious counselors in ever-increasing numbers. A "tort" is a private or civil wrong or injury (as opposed to a criminal act), other than a contract dispute, for which the law will allow monetary damages. Generally, this wrong involves a violation of a commonly accepted duty. (*Black's*, 1979, 1335). A counselee will bring a tort suit against the religious counselor, alleging negligent acts or omissions, and perhaps also alleging intentional acts.

To prevail in a negligence action, one must prove that (1) the minister has a specific duty to protect the counselee; (2) the minister failed to fulfill that duty; (3) the minister's failure caused the injury in question; and (4) the injury resulted in actual harm to the counselee. For example, the religious counselor has a duty to tend to icy office steps that counselees will have to mount in the winter; areas under his/her control must be maintained in such a way as to minimize harm to others. Failing to remove or abate such a dangerous condition would normally be viewed as a breach of the duty to maintain safe premises, particularly as the premises are open to the public.

Professional Malpractice

Bringing an action for negligence means proving that a normal person's conduct has fallen below a minimum standard. (Keeton, 1984, 185–193). On the other hand, when someone has superior knowledge or intelligence, the law requires that he/she act in accordance with that knowledge. Professionals who have special skills, training, and expertise, and who fail to adhere to a higher standard than the average citizen are liable in tort for professional malpractice. (*Id.*)

Considering the principles of professional malpractice, a court would need to decide whether the pastor who does counseling would be held to a general standard set by (1) secular counselors; (2) ministers generally or of one's specific denomination; or (3) full-time pastoral counselors (however that term may be defined). Answering this question has engendered great debate among courts, scholars, and church professionals.

Clergy Malpractice: *Nally* and Its Lessons

Insurance Companies "Predict" the Future

It has been alleged that the insurance industry tried to create a perceived need for clergy malpractice insurance by reporting falsely in 1979 that, for the first time ever, a pastor had been sued for clergy malpractice. (Breecher, 1980, 15–17). Hoping to foster a desire for such insurance, it was reported to the media that a clergyman had advised a woman in a counseling session to leave her husband. The enraged husband tried to kill his wife after she left him. Sometime thereafter, the couple reconciled and brought suit against the minister, alleging clergy malpractice. One year after this allegedly falsified story was released to the media, the first clergy malpractice case was filed.

Kenneth Nally

In one of the most extraordinary cases to wind its way through the state court system, *Nally v. Grace Community Church* (1984) reveals the palpable uncertainty and disagreement surrounding this area of the law.

Pursuant to the court records, Kenneth Nally was a star baseball player in high school and graduated second in his high school class. He was, however, a troubled student who had previously exhibited suicidal tendencies. As a sophomore at UCLA in 1973, Nally converted from Catholicism to Protestantism and started attending Grace Community Church of the Valley (GCC). GCC had a membership of ten thousand and provided the counseling services of thirty to fifty ministers. Religious counseling was a very important part of the church's ministry, and the church offered these services to a large number of nonmembers as well as members.

Nally's conversion was a source of tension in his family, as he started to make anti-Catholic statements around the home. A friendship formed between Nally and Pastor Cory from GCC. Nally mentioned suicide to Cory and discussed the problems he was having in his relationships with women and his family. Cory advised Nally to get counseling from other ministers at GCC, and Nally's counseling relationship with GCC stretched over a five-year period. In 1975, Nally was seeing a psychologist, as well.

After graduating from UCLA in 1976, Nally attended Logos Bible Institute at GCC. In 1978, Nally started a counseling relationship with Pastor Rea, one of the pastors at GCC. Rea had not had any graduate or undergraduate training in psychology and held no license in any mental health profession. He considered himself gifted in counseling, however. Rea's counseling was biblical; he believed that the Bible contains answers to emotional problems.

In December of 1978, Nally and a girlfriend broke up, and several months thereafter Nally told his mother he was unable to cope with life. She arranged for him to see two doctors. In March of 1979, Nally attempted suicide with an overdose of an antidepressant drug prescribed by one of the doctors who had been treating him.

Nally was comatose when he was admitted to the hospital. A doctor stated to Nally's parents that Nally was still suicidal. Pastors Cory and Rea visited Nally and advised him to cooperate with the psychiatrists at the hospital. Nally told Rea that he would attempt to commit suicide again if given the chance. When Rea was later asked why he did not relay this information to the doctors or to the family, he stated that this would be like going to a fire, seeing the firefighters there, and calling the fire department. Rea's reasons for nondisclosure had nothing to do with the obligation of confidentiality.

Nally told MacArthur, the Senior Pastor of GCC, that he was sorry that he had not been successful in his attempt at suicide. MacArthur did not repeat this comment to anyone. On March 16, 1979, a psychiatrist met with Nally and his father, recommending psychiatric hospitalization as had another doctor who had been working with Nally at the hospital. Nally's parents resisted the idea. It was decided that Nally would be treated on an outpatient basis.

Nally was released and went to stay with Pastor MacArthur because of tension at his family's home. Nally's father at this time overheard MacArthur resist the idea that Nally should see a psychiatrist. Nally was encouraged by MacArthur, however, to attend outpatient treatment. Nally told a friend that he did not want to seek the help of a doctor or psychiatrist because they were not Christian.

Pastor Thomson, another pastor at GCC, arranged for Nally to have a complete physical exam. Thomson told Nally, in response to a question, that if Nally committed suicide, he would still be accepted into heaven. Pastor MacArthur also arranged for Nally to see a doctor. This doctor recommended immediate psychiatric hospitalization. Nally refused and then skipped an outpatient appointment. This doctor called Nally's father, offering to send an ambulance, but both parents were reluctant.

Between March 26 and March 29, 1979, Nally saw three doctors and a psychologist. Nally stated to his father, after seeing the psychologist, that the psychologist would not be able to help Nally because the psychologist was not a good Christian. On March 30, Nally told his girlfriend that he was going to kill himself. She told Pastor Cory. On March 31, Nally had a dispute with his family. On April 1, at the age of twenty-four, Nally was found in a friend's apartment with a fatal, self-inflicted gunshot wound to the head.

Grieving Parents

Nally's parents brought suit against GCC, Pastor MacArthur, Pastor Rea, Pastor Cory, and Pastor Thomson for one million dollars in damages. *(Nally,* 1984). The complaint alleges, in count one, titled clergy malpractice, that MacArthur as an agent for the church provided spiritual and personal counseling to Nally, that he discouraged Nally from receiving psychiatric or psychological counseling although he was aware that Nally had suicidal tendencies, and that Nally committed suicide because he did not receive essential psychiatric or psychological care and treatment.

The parents alleged that MacArthur obtained the confidence of and exercised influence and control over their son. Despite his knowledge of the severe nature of Nally's suicidal tendencies, MacArthur counseled Nally to consult with lay counselors on the staff of the church, pray, read the Scriptures, and listen to tape recordings of MacArthur's sermons. The parents alleged that MacArthur failed to make himself available to Nally when requested. As such, MacArthur failed to exercise the standard of care for a clergy person of his sect and training, which resulted in Nally's suicide.

In count two, titled negligence, the parents alleged that the GCC and Pastor MacArthur negligently failed to require the proper level of psychological training for their church counselors.

In the third count, titled outrageous conduct, the parents alleged that each of the named pastors intentionally inflicted emotional distress on Nally by exacerbating his preexisting feelings of guilt, anxiety, and depression, knowing that Nally had suicidal tendencies and that their conduct would increase the likelihood that Nally would take his own life.

Although the defendants knew that Nally had a family background of Catholicism, the defendants ridiculed, disparaged, and denigrated the Catholic religion and faith, stating that Catholics were not Christians and would not go to heaven at death. The parents alleged that the defendants convinced Nally that he had betrayed Christ's love and trust. They isolated him and prevented his contact with people outside of the church. These acts were done with reckless disregard for the health, safety, and well-being of Nally, and as a result, Nally's depression increased, causing him to commit suicide.

In response, the defendants alleged, among other things, that the free exercise clause and the establishment clause protected them from such a suit. The court agreed with the church and the pastors, and dismissed the suit without a trial.

The Evidence Evaluated on Appeal

Nally's parents filed an appeal, and the court of appeals reviewed the evidence. (*Nally*, 1984). The parents introduced evidence from an expert that the defendants increased Nally's despair and anguish. Indeed, this expert testified that the attitude and naïveté of the members of GCC toward someone as severely disturbed as Nally was incomprehensible.

MacArthur had stated that counseling like the type he had with Nally caused "the deepest depression." After the first suicide attempt, Nally's arm was paralyzed. The pastors had told him that this was a sign that God was punishing him. Nally's father stated that a few days after Nally's attempted suicide, he opened the door to interrupt Cory's counseling session with his son and found Nally on his knees, crying. Pastor Rea admitted to Nally's father after the suicide that this was not the first suicide of someone involved in the church.

Further evidence included a tape recording made by Pastor Thomson entitled "Principles of Biblical Counseling"; it inferred that suicide was an acceptable, even preferable, alternative if one could not overcome his/her sinful nature. This tape was designed for the counselors at GCC, and all of the defendants used the same counseling techniques. Thomson admitted that for religious reasons he did not refer his counselees to psychologists or psychiatrists. He believed that an answer from a secular counselor was less than God's goal and the Bible gave the root answer to emotional and psychiatric problems.

The Legal Issues of the First Appeal

The court of appeals stated that it had to determine whether a clergy person should be immune from liability for intentional infliction of emotional distress caused by the nature or content of counseling simply because the counseling may have a spiritual aspect. The court reviewed a case where excessive child punishment was not privileged from prosecution despite the fact that it was imposed under the guise of religious expression. The court also reviewed a case where an action was maintained against a priest for false imprisonment despite the fact that the imprisonment was religiously motivated. Shocking the law schools and rocking the religious profession, the court held that the record before the lower court did not establish that the ministers did not engage in intentional infliction of emotional distress and, therefore, the case would be remanded back to the lower court for a thorough review of this issue. It had been generally expected that the court would find the ministers immune from suit based on the religion clauses.

One judge wrote a strong and lengthy dissent, stating that the facts simply did not support allegations that the church intentionally or recklessly brought about Nally's suicide. The church and the pastors appealed to the highest court in the state, the California Supreme Court. The court declined to review the case; however, it nullified the court of appeals decision and sent the case to the lower court for a trial.

The Trial

A three-week trial ensued. The Nallys introduced witnesses regarding pastoral care standards. The trial court would not allow a witness from the American Pastoral Counseling Association [*sic*] to testify, finding "that the group had not been accepted by the general pastoral counseling community as experts in the field of pastoral counseling," and because the defendants did not belong to the association. At the end of the trial, the court ruled that the Nallys had produced no evidence upon which a jury could find a verdict for them. By entering this decision, the court avoided all issues regarding the viability of a clergy malpractice claim or the application of First Amendment defenses.

The Second Appeal

Clergy Malpractice or Negligence?

The Nallys appealed the decision. (*Nally*, 1987). Refusing to decide whether Nally's evidence was sufficient to prevail, the appellate court simply reversed the trial court's finding of no evidence. The court determined that counselors in California, religious or not, must refer mentally disturbed suicidal youth to those authorized and best suited to prevent imminent suicide. Referral would be to one authorized by state law either to prescribe medication or initiate involuntary hospitalization. The appeals court specified that the duty entailed, at a minimum, telling the counselee to see a psychotherapist or psychiatrist and perhaps informing loved ones. By analogy, the court relied upon a case involving a hotel that had a history of guests jumping from its windows. In that case, the court decided that the hotel failed in its duty to prevent suicide where a woman checking in exhibited bizarre behavior.

Clarifying that it was not upholding the tort of clergy malpractice, the court stated that it was phrasing the suit as one for "negligently failing to prevent suicide and intentional infliction of emotional injury causing suicide." The court distinguished "pastoral counselors" from psychiatrists and licensed psychotherapists. Accordingly, although the court determined that "pastoral counselors" are nontherapist counselors, it held that even nontherapist counselors must take appropriate measures to minimize the likelihood of suicide. A counselee develops a dependence on a counselor, the court reasoned, regardless of the specifics or variations of the individual's training or religious perspective.

The court reviewed and relied upon the intent of the California legislature as evidenced by specific laws distinguishing between the religious confessor and the pastoral counselor. The former is protected by privileges of confidentiality, and the latter is not. Moreover, the California legislature had specifically created a psychotherapist-patient privilege that again is not extended to the pastoral counselor. Thus, requiring a psychotherapist to warn or inform others would derogate from the confidentiality intended by the state legislature. Requiring pastoral counselors to warn, however, would not. In addition, a psychiatrist is legally authorized to institutionalize the suicide-prone patient or prescribe medication. Requiring a psychiatrist to warn or inform would not place the patient in the hands of anyone more competent. Ideally, a nontherapist's referral would place the counselee under the care of one specially authorized to prevent suicide.

The court stated that it was not requiring pastoral counselors to abandon their counselees. Nor would pastoral counselors be liable for continuing religious counseling with a suicidal counselee; instead, they would need to augment their work with one specially recognized by state statute as being authorized to act in this area. Additionally, GCC would have a duty to train its pastoral counselors to learn how to recognize the suicidal counselee, to know their responsibilities in this area, and to be knowledgeable about referral.

The First Amendment

The court reviewed the First Amendment concerns, determining that referring to, or informing, others in a position to help would not interfere with the counselor's religious beliefs. Indeed, referral could be consistent with the practice of referring only to Christian psychotherapists. The court discussed the state's interest in preserving life and stated that the "lives of mentally disturbed people who happen to go to a pastoral counselor are just as precious as those who go to a psychiatrist or some other mental health practitioner." As such, the liability would not be the result of engaging in religious counseling but in failing to discharge other duties owed to the counselee.

Under the court's ruling, no court would ever need to judge or probe the content of the pastor's counseling because the duty to refer would exist independent of and in addition to the pastor's normal counseling care. The court concluded by stating that it had not created a broad-gauged action for clergy malpractice; instead, it had refused to create a new broad-gauged defense of clergy immunity. The court returned the case to the lower court, stating that the lower court had been wrong to find that there was no evidence to support the Nallys' claims.

One member of the panel, Justice Cole, wrote a strong dissent, accusing the majority of making law as opposed to interpreting it. Cole called the court's ruling impracticable, unwieldy, and vague. He asserted that it is impossible to determine where spirituality ends and psychology begins.

The Church and the Pastors Appeal

Rather than allow the case to return to the lower court, the defendants appealed to the state's Supreme Court. (*Nally,* 1988). All of California's Supreme Court Justices participated. In a dramatic decision, the court reversed the court of appeals and affirmed the trial court. The court determined that "pastoral counselors" are not professional counselors and as such cannot be required to conform to professional conduct. Indeed, the court quoted MacArthur as stating that GCC did not have a professional counseling ministry, despite the fact that the Nallys introduced evidence that GCC advertised its counselors as competent to treat a myriad of emotional problems and as able to look with full confidence to God's Word for the counselee's proper solution. Several counselors had testified that they considered themselves fully competent to treat a whole range of mental illnesses, including depression and schizophrenia.

The court noted the age of Nally and the fact that he voluntarily entered into the counseling relationship, which was noncommercial and noncustodial. A pastoral counselor is a nonprofessional source of guidance, the court determined, quite distinct from a licensed mental health professional. And, although therapists may have a duty to protect innocent third parties from their client's harm, there was no duty to protect the counselee from self-inflicted harm.

Imposition of a duty to refer on nontherapists would unduly burden them and would stifle gratuitous, religious counseling. For instance, counselees might be deterred from seeking help out of fear that they might be subjected to involuntary commitment to psychiatric facilities. The court concluded that to hold the defendants responsible would place blame unreasonably. It stated, however, that if a nontherapist counselor held him/herself out as a professional, he/she would be liable for injuries related to his/her counseling activities.

Two judges disagreed with the majority, finding that a duty to refer must be imposed on pastoral counselors; that is, pastoral counselors have a duty simply to recognize the limits of their own competence to treat an individual. Nonetheless, they agreed with the result of the opinion because, after weighing the evidence, they found that the pastors had not contributed significantly to Nally's suicide and had fulfilled their duty to refer him to medical and psychological doctors.

The Litigation Concludes

The Nallys appealed the adverse decision to the United States Supreme Court. Almost nine years from the day that the Nallys first filed suit against GCC and almost exactly ten years from the date of their son's suicide, the High Court declined to review the case, bringing all litigation to a close.

Aftermath

Nally Has Resulted in a Turf War

Some argue that *Nally* sets up a hierarchy of qualified and competent counselors of which religious counselors are not even included. That is, if a person wants or needs "real" help, he/she must go to someone recognized by the state as competent. That leaves religious counselors in a standardless and somewhat irrelevant profession. Thus, although some view *Nally* as a clear victory for the church because the court found that the profession was not responsible to the state (i.e., the public) for its counseling, others saw the clergy in our society being shunted more and more to the periphery. *Nally* sanctions the assumption that licensed counselors are more effective than and superior to religious counselors in preventing suicide. (Slater, 1989, 937); (Sacramento, 1987); (McCaffrey, 1990, 160).

Some writers have argued, partially tongue in cheek, after *Nally*, that secular counselors should have a duty to refer their clients to religious counselors. (Ericsson, 1981, 175); (McCaffrey, 1990, 148 [citing Gorsuch,

1988]); (Kramer, 1988). For two thousand years, pastors, priests, rabbis, and other spiritual counselors have been providing solace for those suffering from guilt, anxiety, and depression. (Ericsson, 1981, 166). Freud and Jung both admitted that "we psychotherapists must occupy ourselves with problems which, strictly speaking, belong to the theologian." (Burek, 1986, 139 [quoting Szasz, 1975]). In *Nally*, neither the secular counselors nor the medical doctors were effective in preventing Nally's untimely death. Even psychiatrists admit, "To date psychiatry has not clearly defined the skills, knowledge, and attitudes that the psychiatrists in training must demonstrate in order to be certified as competent." (Ericsson, 1981, 171 [quoting Weinstein and Russell, 1976]).

The Future of Clergy Malpractice

To date, no one has been found liable for clergy malpractice. Questions that a court would have to address in recognizing the claim of clergy malpractice are so numerous and daunting that it is doubtful that a court will ever undertake to answer them. Instead, the courts will find ministers liable under the basic torts of invasion of privacy, breach of fiduciary duty, or outrageous conduct.

In all likelihood, the courts will eschew making a judgment as to proper and normative clergy conduct because defining clergy malpractice would necessitate excessive entanglement with religion. Religious counselors have no uniform education, testing, licensing, or practices. Additionally, religious counselors may have many functions in the church, of which counseling is only one. It may not be fair to analogize to other professionals like the psychologist, who is trained exclusively in and is expected to be competent only in the area of counseling. (Fiorillo, 1987).

References

Black's Law Dictionary. (1979). (5th ed.). St. Paul: West Publishing Co.

Breecher, M. M. (1980). Ministerial Malpractice. *Liberty, March-April,* 15–17.

Burek, L. M. (1986). Clergy Malpractice: Making Clergy Accountable to a Lower Power. *Pepperdine Law Review, 14,* 137–161.

Ericsson, S. E. (1981). Clergyman Malpractice: Ramifications of a New Theory. *Valparaiso University Law Review, 16,* 163–184.

Fiorillo, M. J. (1987). Clergy Malpractice: Should Pennsylvania Recognize a Cause of Action for Improper Counseling by a Clergyman? *Dickinson Law Review, 92,* 223–251.

Gorsuch, R., & Meylink, W. D. (1988, Fall). Toward a Co-Professional Model of Clergy-Psychologist Referral. *Journal of Psychology and Christianity, 7,* 22–31.

Keeton, W. P. (1984 & Supp. 1988). *Prosser and Keeton on the Law of Torts* (5th ed.). St. Paul: West Publishing Co.

Kramer, W. (1988, July 5). The "Nally" Case Could Put a Severe Chill on Clergy Counseling. *Los Angeles Daily Journal, 101,* 4.

McCaffrey, C. G. (1990). Nally v. Grace Community Church of the Valley: Clergy Malpractice—A Threat to Both Liberty and Life. *Pace Law Review, 11,* 137–166.

Nally v. Grace Community Church, 157 Cal. App. 3d 912, 204 Cal. Rptr. 303 (1984), *appeal after remand,* 194 Cal. App. 3d 1147, 240 Cal. Rptr. 215 (1987), *rev'd,* 47 Cal. App. 3d 278, 763 P.2d 948, 253 Cal. Rptr. 97 (1988), *cert. denied,* 490 U.S. 1007 (1989).

Sacramento Bee. (1987, October 28). Case of the Negligent Pastor. *Los Angeles Daily Journal, 100,* 4.

Slater, G. (1989). Nally v. Grace Community Church of the Valley: Absolution for Clergy Malpractice? *Brigham Young University Law Review, 1989,* 913–942.

Szasz, T. S. (1975). The Theology of Therapy: The Breach of the First Amendment Through the Medicalization of Morals. *New York University Review of Law and Social Change, 5,* 127–135.

Weinstein, H. M., & Russell, M. L. (1976, August). Competency-Based Psychiatric Education. *American Journal of Psychiatry, 133,* 935–939.

3

THE EXPANDING VULNERABILITY OF RELIGIOUS COUNSELORS TO LEGAL ACTION: SEXUAL MISCONDUCT AND THE DUTY TO PROTECT THIRD PARTIES

The best knower of the human soul will be the one who has lived through passions himself.

—Alfred Adler

Introduction

In recent years, the types of conduct for which clergy (religious counselors) are sued and the theories upon which liability has been based have broadened. Several areas of religious counseling are subject to increased liability or legal regulation. Even though no state has yet hung religious negligence upon the specific peg of "clergy malpractice," states have increasingly set sanctions for counselor sexual exploitation and the duty to protect third parties from the dangerous acts of counselees.

The social and legal reasons that clergy are increasingly susceptible to legal action can be classified into two categories. First, citizens are increasingly using the courts as a way of addressing grievances. In the past, it was thought that religious people should avoid bringing another to court. Indeed, many believe that it is sacrilegious to bring someone (especially a pastor) to court. Although it is no secret that lawsuits are costly, rancorous, and often unsatisfying affairs, American justice is based upon the ability of everyone to seek redress through the courts.

The primary reason that American jurisprudence encourages civil lawsuits is to discourage citizens from taking the law into their own hands to settle arguments. Alexander Hamilton, one of the chief architects of the constitution for the federalists, was shot and killed by Aaron Burr in a duel to resolve a personal dispute. In many ways, it may be wiser and more civilized to use lawsuits over other methods.

The increase in lawsuits against clergy signals the "mainstreaming" of the profession into the norms and difficulties of other professional groups. Social workers, lawyers, physicians, psychologists, and other professionals are increasingly affected by the same litigious environment.

Clergy must now face the legal consequences for professional negligence or intentional wrongdoing that are imposed upon other professional groups. This leads to the second reason for the increased lawsuits against clergy.

Clergy are increasingly vulnerable to liability because they may well be the least prepared for their professional roles in terms of their legal training. A nonrandom sample of theological schools indicates that few courses are offered to prepare religious counselors for the variety of clinical situations that may lead to lawsuits. Thus, clergy are increasingly faced with legal issues that previous generations of clergy have not had to address.

Criminal Sexual Conduct and Religious Counselors

Four states have enacted laws making sexual misconduct a *civil* offense. These include California, Illinois, Minnesota, and Wisconsin. Wisconsin and Minnesota specifically include clergy; California and Illinois include clergy by implication. Additionally, a growing number of states have passed *criminal* laws specifically prohibiting therapists from engaging in sexual relations with counselees. These include California (1990), Colorado (1990), Florida (1991), Georgia (1992), Iowa (1992), Maine (1991), Minnesota (1992), North Dakota (1989), and Wisconsin (1990). The Iowa, Minnesota, North Dakota, and Wisconsin statutes specifically include religious professionals. The others mentioned above may be construed to include the religious professional.

These statutes can be illustrated by the Florida law (§ 491.0112), which states:

> (1) Any psychotherapist who commits sexual misconduct with a client, or former client when the professional relationship was terminated primarily for the purpose of engaging in sexual contact, commits a felony in the third degree.
> (2) Any psychotherapist who violates [the above statute] by means of therapeutic deception commits a felony in the second degree.

Generally, these statutes have several points in common. First, the caregiver is called generically the "psychotherapist." The term "psychotherapist" may be broad enough to include both religious counselors who are licensed counselors and those who are not. Although Iowa, Minnesota, North Dakota, and Wisconsin specifically define members of the clergy as "psychotherapists" for the purposes of their statutes, virtually all of the other statutes include those persons who "purport" to conduct counseling. A nonlicensed, religious counselor who suggests to a counselee that he/she is a counselor or that he/she can provide counseling services fulfills the definition for the purposes of these laws and is liable and accountable under the statute.

The Wisconsin statute (§ 940.22[2]) illustrates the elements of this crime:

> Any person who is or who holds himself or herself out to be a therapist and who intentionally has sexual contact with a patient or client during any on-going therapist-client or therapist-patient relationship regardless of whether it occurs during any treatment, consultation, interview or examination, is guilty of a class D felony. Consent is not an issue in an action under this subsection.

The second element that these statutes have in common is that "consent" is *not* a defense to this crime. States, generally, do not criminalize sexual acts between "consenting" adults beyond adultery and homosexual acts. After the age of majority, people are responsible for their own decisions regarding consensual sexual acts. Sexual behavior of people past the age of majority, however, will be criminalized if it involves a person who is mentally incapacitated, mentally deficient, or physically helpless. Thus, these statutes constitute a new, unique protection for adults entering the counselor-counselee relationship. Society is recognizing the vulnerability of those who enter into counseling.

The third element of commonality in the statutes is that the definition of "sexual misconduct" is generally broad and includes a wide range of sexual behavior. The statutes criminalize two classes of sexual misconduct: sexual intercourse and sexual contact. The Wisconsin statute (§ 940.225[5]) provides clear and forthright definitions typical of these statutes:

> "Sexual intercourse" includes . . . cunnilingus, fellatio or anal intercourse between persons or any other intrusions, however slight, of any part of a person's body or of any object into the genital or anal opening either by the defendant or upon the defendant's instruction. The emission of semen is not required.

Also typical of these statutes is the broad, inclusive definition of prohibited sexual contact. Wisconsin (§ 940.225[5][b]) provides such an illustration:

> "Sexual contact" means any intentional touching by the complainant or defendant, either directly or through clothing by the use of any body part or object, of the complainant's or defendant's intimate parts if that intentional touching is either for the purpose of sexually degrading; or for the purpose of sexually humiliating the complainant or sexually arousing or gratifying the defendant or if the touching contains the elements of sexual battery.

The final point worth noting is that Florida, Colorado, and Minnesota include "therapeutic deception" as an element to this crime. Florida defines this term as a "representation to the client that sexual contact by the psychotherapist is consistent with or part of the treatment of the client." This definition means that the clergy-therapist cannot express or imply that sexual activity with the counselor will help resolve the counselee's sexual or personal problems. Minnesota requires evidence that the counselee was "emotionally dependent" upon the counselor before therapeutic deception can be established.

Recently, a Minnesota court had the opportunity to apply the therapist-client sexual exploitation statute and its elements of "therapeutic deception" and "emotional dependency." (*State v. Dutton,* 1990). Robert Dutton was convicted at trial of four counts of criminal psychotherapist-patient sexual conduct. In 1985, he approached a female and her husband about joining his church. The woman testified that she went to Pastor Dutton for counseling regarding low self-esteem and suicidal thoughts, among other things. Dutton said he could not help her as much as a Christian psychologist and he would soon refer her. Nonetheless, he continued the sessions and repeatedly asked questions about the woman's sexuality. At the close of one of the sessions, Dutton hugged the counselee, and by the next session they engaged in hugging and "passionate kissing."

The physical relationship developed into a sexual relationship in April of 1986, when Dutton touched the woman's intimate parts ostensibly to help her to work out negative feelings about her sexuality. The next month they engaged in sexual intercourse—with Dutton representing that this sexual relationship would be more beneficial than sexual relations with her husband because Dutton was "unselfish."

After this initial sexual encounter, the woman became dangerously dependent upon Dutton. In a document, she wrote, "I, the undersigned have given Robert E. Dutton control of my life—my future out of my abiding love for him." Additionally, during their relationship, the woman signed over $11,000 to Dutton and sent him thirty-two cards and letters. During the period in which Dutton had sex with his counselee, he told her that sexual activity with him would "free" her from being hung up sexually and that it was God's response to her desire to be asexual.

Dutton appealed his conviction on the grounds that the evidence did not support the elements of "emotional dependency" and "therapeutic deception." The court of appeals dismissed Dutton's assertions and sustained his conviction. The court found that the counselee exhibited emotional dependence in the number of cards, letters, and money sent to Dutton as well as signing her "life" over to him. Also, the court found that Dutton "therapeutically deceived" his counselee by "methodically" asserting that sexual relations with him would have therapeutic value.

The court found that pastors come within the "psychotherapist" definition for the purposes of this statute. It seems clear that Dutton represented himself to be a therapist to his counselee and continued to act as if his ministrations to her had therapeutic value and rationale.

Society is becoming increasingly more sophisticated in understanding the psychodynamics of counseling relationships. The appellate court approved of expert testimony at trial from two licensed psychologists and a pastoral counselor. These witnesses testified that Dutton's counselee suffered from a "dependent personality disorder" and that she "idealized" Dutton. Their relationship was characterized by an unfair and untherapeutic power imbalance. The court's ruling made it clear that Dutton should have recognized this power imbalance and, at the very least, done nothing to exploit it. The goal of counseling sessions with a dependent personality person is to help build the counselee's inner strength and stability. The court found that Dutton not only failed in his duty to build his counselee's strength and stability but exploited the very weaknesses that brought the counselee to him in the first place.

Clarifying the criminal statute further, a Minnesota court ruled in another case on the boundaries of physical touching. The counselee charged that a pastor gave her a hug during a counseling session and pressed her breasts into his chest. The appeals court, affirming the trial court, ruled that "hugging" was not the kind of "touching" that the Minnesota criminal statute intended to outlaw; "[a]n ordinary hug . . . seeks to convey and promote an attitude of affection" (*State v. Ohrtman*, 1991, 4). Here, the court had to draw a legal distinction between an affectionate hug and an illegal, exploitive hug.

Psychosocial Dynamics in Clergy Sexual Misconduct

"Transference" is increasingly recognized by courts as a factor in sexual misconduct. The *Dutton* case focused on transference as an operative factor in holding clergy liable for sexual misconduct. According to the transference phenomenon, the counselee imposes feelings and thoughts about a person in the counselee's life upon the counselor. For example, a counselee's feelings about a parent are often imposed upon the "parental" figure of the therapist. Countertransference refers to the projections that the counselor imposes onto the counselee. Properly handled, transference can have therapeutic value. If transferences are improperly handled by the professional, they can lead both to legal and therapeutic disaster.

Such transferences are dangerous for two reasons. First, transferences distort both religious and therapeutic judgment. Second, in unredeemed or mishandled transference, each party becomes an object. Where the counselee projects onto the religious professional the longed-for warmth of a parent, the religious counselor is depersonalized into the graven image of the counselee's own making. The religious professional who does not resist this identification—or those who use it to gain power over their counselees—perpetuates a sick and dangerous charade. Such charades are increasingly unmasked by courts. Transferences involving religious professionals can be particularly intense because of the "parental," even "Godly," associations with the clerical role.

Gutheil (1989) asserts that counselees diagnosed with borderline personality disorders constitute the majority of those most likely to falsely accuse therapists of sexual misconduct. He states that "borderline personality" counselees tend to confuse and to lose interpersonal boundaries and effectively to manipulate the clinician-client relationship. Gutheil states that this diagnosis is no excuse for counselor misconduct and advises that such counselees pose a warning for religious counselors to be "scrupulous—even overscrupulous" in setting and maintaining boundaries in the professional relationship. Borderline personality disordered individuals are likely to be encountered by religious counselors, for the disorder is "apparently common" among the general population (American Psychiatric Association, 1987).

Religious counselors as well as mental health professionals need skills in diagnosing borderline disordered congregants. Clues in assessing such counselees may be helpful. Borderline personality people often exhibit extreme dependency needs and offer the religious professional a "please, help me—you're my last and only hope" demeanor. Although religious counselors may want to extend aid and comfort to their membership and others, "buying into" the pathological dependency of borderline persons helps no one. Religious professionals need to distinguish between the therapeutic helping and a "helping" that satisfies either a dysfunctional need on the part of a congregant or a need to be a "savior" on the part of the religious counselor.

Another psychosocial dynamic is a new type of addiction called sexual addiction. As the name implies, sexual addiction refers to patterns of sexual fantasy and behavior that increasingly place emotions, finances, social life, marriage, and family at risk. (Earle and Crow, 1990). Warning signs for those at risk of sexual addiction include lapses in efficiency at home or work, rapid and unpredictable mood changes, marked changes in sexual behavior (i.e., extreme interest or aversion in sexual activity), combinations of compulsive behaviors (i.e., alcoholism and gambling, etc.), and a family history of addictive or compulsive behaviors. Although the prevalence of sexual addiction is unknown, religious counselors should be sensitized to its appearance among clients and congregants.

Sexual addiction, either on the part of the religious counselor or counselee, can wreak havoc in counseling. Given the privacy of the religious counseling milieu, therapeutic sessions could degenerate into sessions to share sexual fantasies and sexual liaisons. Additionally, the role of a religious counselor, who represents religious authority and who is often perceived as a nurturing, caring person, may serve as a powerful incentive to act out sexually.

The Duty to Protect Third Parties

In 1981, Mr. Neufang began marital counseling with his minister. Shortly thereafter, he shot his wife, rendering her a paraplegic. Mrs. Neufang, as a third party, brought a suit against the minister, alleging that he was negligent for failing to warn her of her husband's violent emotional state. (Burek, 1986, 142). The court dismissed the case because no special relationship existed between the pastor and Mrs. Neufang.

Generally one is not required to come to the aid of another. The law allows citizens to be heedless of others' needs, requiring only that no harm be done to others. This legal doctrine has one important exception. Where a special relationship exists between people, an obligation to care for them may exist. Courts have carved out a special relationship exception for physician-patient and psychotherapist-client relationships. This duty becomes obvious in the parent-child relationship; that is, because of the special relationship, the parent has a duty to protect and/or rescue his/her child.

The counselor has a special relationship with his/her counselee. This special relationship creates special obligations and duties that the counselor owes to the counselee. For example, to leave the counselee emotionally and psychologically stranded can cause severe harm to the counselee, and such termination may fall below the standard of care. In recent years, this duty extending from the professional to the counselee (the second party) has been expanded to include certain third parties. A third party can be anyone other than the counselee.

In 1976, the Supreme Court of California issued a landmark decision that established a counselor's duty to certain third parties and gained national attention. In 1969, a student at Berkeley, Prosenjit Poddar, began counseling at the university. During this time he disclosed to his counselor that he intended to kill his girlfriend, Tatiana Tarasoff. Poddar did not identify her by name, but she would have been easily identifiable. The psychologist told the campus police of Poddar's intentions; the police took Poddar into custody for questioning, but released him with a warning to stay away from his girlfriend. The head psychiatrist at the counseling center then ordered that no further action be taken regarding Poddar and that all the documentation on his case be destroyed. Two months later Poddar stabbed his girlfriend, Tatiana Tarasoff, to death.

Tatiana Tarasoff's parents sued the psychologist, the police, and the University of California Board of Regents for the wrongful death of their daughter. Tarasoff's parents claimed that the duty of care owed by the counselor to Poddar also should have extended to their daughter (a third party). After many appeals, the California Supreme Court held that psychotherapists have a duty to warn innocent third parties who may be in danger from the psychotherapists' counselees. (*Tarasoff v. Regents of the University of California*, 1976).

Objections from counseling professionals basically fell into two categories: (1) counselors cannot predict with any accuracy when their counselees will harm someone else, and (2) such a warning would undermine the counselor's obligation of confidentiality to the counselee. (Small, 1985). The California Supreme Court was cognizant of these issues and addressed them in its ruling.

First, the court stated that it must be "reasonably foreseeable" that a specific person was in actual danger. Courts seem to be favoring an expansive interpretation of the doctrine of the "foreseeable" third party victim. (Pietrofesa, Pietrofesa, and Pietrofesa, 1990). The third party victim need not be identified by name and address for the duty to apply. For example, a California court held that a young child was a "reasonably foreseeable" victim when the assailant had made up his mind to shoot the young child's mother. (*Hedlund v. Superior Court*, 1983).

Second, the court determined that protecting the public from lethal threats is more important than keeping confidences. Counselors argue that counselees will not fully confide their thoughts if they know that counselors must warn others, thereby undermining the value of therapy.

On the horns of this dilemma, the *Tarasoff* court said that when therapists, using the standards of their profession, determine (or should determine) that their counselee poses a danger to someone else, the therapists are required to use reasonable care to protect others. The court stated that the measures taken by the therapist to protect third parties will vary from case to case.

Subsequent court cases and state law have further delineated who must be warned and under what circumstances. (Fulero, 1988). For example, a federal court found that a psychiatrist's failure to review a patient's medical records amounted to a failure to protect a third party. The medical records would have revealed the patient's history of violence toward women, and a warning to the girlfriend might have prevented her murder. (*Jablonski by Pahls v. United States*, 1983). Generally, the courts have held that therapists do not have a duty to warn a vague "someone"; the threat must be specific and not addressed to society at large. (*Thompson v. County of Alameda*, 1980).

The principles of *Tarasoff* have been adopted and applied in numerous states, including North Carolina (*Currie v. United States*, 1986), Alaska (*Division of Corrections v. Neakok*, 1986), Vermont (*Peck v. Counseling Serv.*, 1985), Kansas (*Durflinger v. Artiles*, 1983), Washington State (*Petersen v. State*, 1983), Indiana (*Estate of Mathes v. Ireland*, 1981), Pennsylvania (*Leedy v. Hartnett*, 1981), Nebraska (*Lipari v. Sears, Roebuck & Co.*, 1980), and New Jersey (*McIntosh v. Milano*, 1979). (Fulero, 1988).

New Hampshire (1984), Montana (1989), and Michigan (1990) have written the duty to warn into their state statutes. The Michigan statute imposes this duty on specifically defined professionals: psychiatrists, psychologists, psychiatric social workers, certified social workers, social workers, and social work technicians. Religious counselors need to ascertain firmly, by examining their state regulations, whether their training or work requirements place them within these professional categories. As mentioned earlier, one court found student chaplains to be, in essence, social workers because their functions and duties were defined under the statute. (*State v. Motherwell*, 1990).

Designated professionals are required to warn third parties where counselees threaten physical violence against a "reasonably identifiable" third person. The duty is discharged by (1) hospitalizing the counselee; (2) making a reasonable attempt to tell the third party of the threat and inform the police; and/or (3) communicating the threat to the department of social services or the legal custodian if the intended victim is a minor.

Cohen (1990) suggested a model for counselors wanting to limit their confidentiality duties to HIV-positive counselees who may pose a danger to third parties. This model is analogous to the dilemma faced by maintaining confidentiality among religious counselors and can be another source of guidance even though not directly applicable. He recommended that the counselor (1) acquire some medical evidence that the counselee has the disease; (2) ascertain that the AIDS person has a relationship to a specific third party such that the medical authorities would believe that the third party was in danger; and (3) determine that the third party is neither already aware of the danger nor is likely to be timely informed by other sources.

Cohen also suggested that, once the above three criteria were satisfied, the disclosure must be done promptly and appropriately. He stated that the HIV-positive counselee should be fully educated about HIV and AIDS, the counselee must be informed that the counselor intends to warn the third party, the warning itself must be made in a timely fashion, the disclosure must be made only to the third party or his/her guardians, the warning must address only the disease, and the counselor must be willing to provide support and appropriate referral to the third party.

Carefully complying with the state statute protects the counselor in three ways. First, Michigan, Montana, and New Hampshire specify that informing third parties does not compromise the counselor's duties of confidentiality. "Counselor" or "therapist," in each statute, are defined terms and do not include clergy. Prudence, however, suggests that religious counselors comply with these statutes. Second, two statutes state explicitly that warning a foreseeable victim immunizes the counselor so that the counselee cannot sue the counselor for breach of contract, libel, slander, or other causes of action. Third, warning foreseeable victims immunizes the counselor from possible suits for failure to warn. Making "reasonable efforts" to notify endangered third parties fulfills the duty to warn.

At least one author, from a legal standpoint, has asserted that requiring clergy to protect third parties is unmanageable if not unwarranted. (Milne, 1986). Milne suggested that because clergy have no universally accepted code of ethics or doctrine and enjoy broad privileged communications and First Amendment protections, clergy are unique and different from other counseling professions. Clearly, when clergy represent themselves as licensed counselors, they should be held to the same standard of care as is any other counseling professional. Whether third parties should receive less protection from religious counselors than is expected of secular counselors is an open question.

References

American Psychiatric Association. (1987). *Diagnostic and Statistical Manual of Mental Disorders.* Washington, D.C.: Author.

Burek, L. M. (1986). Clergy Malpractice: Making Clergy Accountable to a Lower Power. *Pepperdine Law Review, 14,* 137–161.

Cohen, E. D. (1990). Confidentiality, Counseling, and Clients Who Have AIDS: Ethical Foundations of a Model Rule. *Journal of Counseling and Development, 68,* 282–286.

Currie v. United States, 644 F. Supp. 1074 (M.D.N.C. 1986), *aff'd,* 836 F.2d 209 (4th Cir. 1987).

Division of Corrections v. Neakok, 721 P.2d 1121 (Alaska, 1986).

Durflinger v. Artiles, 234 Kan. 484, 673 P.2d 86 (1983).

Earle, R. H., & Crow, G. M. (1990). Sexual Addiction: Understanding and Treating the Phenomenon. *Contemporary Family Therapy, 12*(2), 89–104.

Estate of Mathes v. Ireland, 419 N.E.2d 782 (Ind. 1981).

Florida statute, § 491.0112 (1991).

Fulero, S. M. (1988). Tarasoff: Ten Years Later. *Professional Psychology: Research and Practice, 19*(2), 184–190.

Gutheil, T. G. (1989). Boundary Personality Disorder, Boundary Violations, and Patient-Therapist Sex: Medicolegal Pitfalls. *American Journal of Psychiatry, 146*(5), 597–602.

Hedlund v. Superior Court, 34 Cal. App. 3d 695, 669 P.2d 41, 194 Cal. Rptr. 805 (1983).

Jablonski by Pahls v. United States, 712 F.2d 391 (9th Cir. 1983).

Leedy v. Hartnett, 510 F. Supp. 1125 (M.D. Pa. 1981), *aff'd*, 676 F.2d 686 (3rd Cir. 1982).

Lipari v. Sears, Roebuck & Co., 497 F. Supp. 185 (D. Neb. 1980).

McIntosh v. Milano, 168 N.J. Super. 466, 403 A.2d 500 (1979).

Michigan statute, § 330.1946 (Supp. 1990).

Milne, T. W. (1986). "Bless Me Father, For I Am About to Sin . . .": Should Clergy Counselors Have a Duty to Protect Third Parties? *Tulsa Law Journal, 22,* 139–165.

Montana statute, § 27-1-1101 (1989).

New Hampshire statute, § 330-A:22 (1984).

Peck v. Counseling Serv., 146 Vt. 61, 499 A.2d 422 (1985).

Petersen v. State, 100 Wash. 2d 421, 671 P.2d 230 (1983).

Pietrofesa, J. J., Pietrofesa, C. J., & Pietrofesa, J. D. (1990). The Mental Health Counselor and "Duty to Warn." *Journal of Mental Health Counselor, 12*(2), 129–137.

Small, L. B. (1985). Psychotherapists' Duty to Warn: Ten Years After *Tarasoff. Golden State University Law Review, 15,* 271–300.

State v. Dutton, 450 N.W.2d 189 (Minn. App. 1990).

State v. Motherwell, 114 Wash. 2d 353, 788 P.2d 1066 (1990).

State v. Ohrtman, 466 N.W.2d 1 (Minn. App. 1991).

Tarasoff v. Regents of the University of California, 17 Cal. App. 3d 425, 551 P.2d 334, 131 Cal. Rptr. 14 (1976).

Thompson v. County of Alameda, 27 Cal. App. 3d 741, 614 P.2d 728, 167 Cal. Rptr. 70 (1980).

Wisconsin statute, § 940.225(5) (West Supp. 1990).

4

STATE REGULATION
OF RELIGIOUS COUNSELORS

[T]he aim of the law is not to punish sins, but is to prevent certain external results.

—*Oliver Wendell Holmes*

Introduction

Some states have begun to license "pastoral counselors" as well as other mental health professionals. This chapter outlines the procedure and the law surrounding licensure, including educational requirements, prohibitions against using titles and professional designations improperly, and exemptions from state licensure by counselors in clergy or other ecclesiastical roles. The legal differences between clergy who are licensed and those who are not will be addressed in addition to the increasing standard of care that is legally expected of licensed clergy.

Familiarity with the state licensure laws is important for four reasons. First, states specifically regulate, under certain circumstances, the counseling performed by religious counselors. Second, religious counselors need to be precise when they describe their counseling services or attribute to themselves titles or qualifications that may be reserved only for those who have been licensed. All states specifically regulate advertised counseling services and the titles used by professionals who render counseling services.

Third, both clergy and nonclergy who work for religious or spiritual institutions may erroneously assume that their work is shielded from state regulation, when in fact their work is construed as counseling. As such, it falls within state regulation for purposes of assessing criminal acts, trade name violations, and civil suits.

Fourth, courts may draw an important distinction between religious counselors who are state licensed to perform counseling and those who are not for purposes of privileged communications. This means that certain professional groups are exempted, within certain parameters, from testifying in court. The Supreme Court of New Hampshire addressed this issue in a case dealing with child sexual abuse. The defendant was convicted of felonious sexual assault of his fifteen-year-old daughter. The defendant appealed his conviction on the ground that testimony given at the trial by a minister should not have been allowed. The defendant claimed that any information the minister received during counseling was "privileged" and could not be given in court.

The court held that testimony by the pastor was properly admitted at trial. (*State v. Melvin*, 1989). The court noted that the privileged communication statute for *certified* pastoral counselors expressly broadened the privilege to operate even when extraneous persons were present during the counseling session. The absence of such a provision in the *uncertified* clergy privilege communication statute therefore could be interpreted only as disallowing the privilege.

Why Licensing for Religious Counselors?

States regulate and license counselors under a variety of professional designations and titles in order to assure that the public has both ethical and competent counselors. State licensing restricts the use of certain titles and establishes requirements for those who use counseling titles.

These statutes precisely formulate the educational, experiential, supervisorial, and ethical requirements expected of counselors. The purposes for licensure are often cited in the licensing statutes themselves. For instance, a Delaware statute (1987) states:

> The primary objective of the Board of Professional Counselors, to which all other objectives and purposes are secondary, is to protect the general public (specifically those persons who are direct recipients of services regulated by this chapter) from unsound practices and from counseling practices which tend to reduce competition or fix the price of services rendered. The secondary objectives of the Board are to maintain minimum standards of practitioner competency and to maintain certain standards in the delivery of services to the public.

California (1990) defines its purposes for regulation of counselors as follows:

> (a) Many California families and many individual Californians are experiencing difficulty and distress, and are in need of wise, competent, caring, compassionate, and effective counseling in order to enable them to improve and maintain healthy family relationships.

These policy statements express the values of the respective state legislatures. Although Delaware expresses its intent to safeguard the public,

California expresses its desire to promote family and personal integrity and well-being.

State licensing requirements have been challenged on constitutional grounds with mixed results. A licensed marriage and family counselor filed suit, claiming that Nevada's prohibitions against the advertising of costs and availability of services were an unconstitutional infringement of her commercial free speech. She had placed ads stating that counseling services were available on a sliding fee scale from $0 to $300 per session. The federal court held that state prohibitions against advertising were illegal. (*Family Counseling Serv. v. Rust*, 1978).

On the other hand, regulations that insured accuracy in advertising were upheld by the Supreme Court of Utah. (*Magleby v. State*, 1977). A licensed marriage and family counselor advertised in the yellow pages that he operated a "center" for human communication even though he was a solo practitioner. The state had adopted the regulations promulgated by the American Association of Marriage and Family Counselors. This advertisement offended the regulations on two counts. The term "center" must denote a group of at least three professionals; moreover, the practitioner's name must not appear in a style and type that sets his/her name above others.

Table 4.1, located at the end of this chapter, shows the state-by-state regulations that apply to mental health counselors. Religious counselors may review their own legal status in light of these professional categories. These represent the licensed counseling professionals for each state. The legend at the top of the table gives the full name for each professional designation (e.g., L.P.C.= Licensed Professional Counselor). The table indicates the statute citation for each state and the minimum educational levels to fulfill the licensure requirements. State requirements for supervised counseling experience and licensing examinations and fees are omitted due to lack of space. Given the nature of licensure statutes as well as other laws to change rapidly, the reader is reminded that each state's licensure statute must be currently examined.

Connecticut, Maine, Michigan, New Hampshire, New Jersey, and Utah specifically allow theological education to fulfill the educational requirements for counseling licensure. Many states allow master's programs "primarily" or "equivalently" in counseling to fulfill the educational requirements.

Each state is free to impose licensing requirements on distinct areas of specialization. Two states (Maine and New Hampshire) have created a separate designation for "pastoral counselor." Each of these states specifically defines the specialization. For example:

"Pastoral counselor" means an individual who is trained and certified

46

to provide for a fee, monetary, or otherwise, pastoral counseling, which is ministry to individuals, families, couples, groups, organizations and the general public involving the application of principles and procedures of counseling to assess and treat intrapersonal and interpersonal problems and other dysfunctional behavior of a social and spiritual nature, and to assist in the overall development and healing process of those served. (Maine, 1990).

States can delineate the requirements for those using the title "pastoral counselor" just as they do for the titles of "clinical social worker," "licensed professional counselor," or other mental health professional titles.

Religious counselors must not state expressly or even imply that they are "pastoral counselors" unless they have been licensed. Indeed, religious counselors must be careful not to give the impression that they have fulfilled the state requirements for pastoral counselors or that they can provide services equivalent to those provided by state-licensed counselors. Finally, religious counselors cannot use titles such as L.P.C. or L.C.S.W. without being licensed in those categories. The religious counselor must walk a fine, clear line between assuring that his or her services are competent, while clarifying that his or her services are not equivalent to those offered by state-regulated counseling professions.

State-regulated titles are not the same as designations from professional organizations. For example, a religious counselor can be a member of the American Association of Pastoral Counselors and still be unable to use the designation "pastoral counselor" within those states regulating that title. Even those who have passed the requirements for membership in the above association or the Association for Clinical Pastoral Education still must fulfill the state requirements if the state regulates that title. Essentially, each state clearly defines the counseling activities that counselors may legally conduct. Religious counselors need to consult their specific state's statutes for such specific regulations and requirements.

When Do States Exempt Religious Counselors from Obtaining Licensure?

Table 4.2, located at the end of this chapter, delineates each state's exemptions to licensing laws, including exemptions for religious counselors. The table sets forth the statute citation and the pertinent statutory text for each exemption. Those state statutes that specifically exempt "clergy" from licensing requirements are noted verbatim. The exemptions listed in Table 4.2 generally correspond to the licensing requirements in Table 4.1. If a state has no explicit exemption, religious counselors may avail themselves of the First Amendment protections for religious counseling. In those states, religious counselors should not overreach their counseling prerogatives; indeed, they should provide counseling within the strictest norms of their denomination and job description.

Exemptions for religious counselors are important because they specifically limit the manner in which religious counselors can advertise, or in any way promote, their counseling services. Religious counselors must obtain licensure when their counseling activities fall outside the narrow exemptions.

Generally, the religious counselor's exemptions from licensure requirements rest on four factors.

1. The religious counselor is ordained, licensed, or otherwise recognized by his/her denomination or sect.
2. The religious counselor is under the supervision of or control of his/her respective denomination or sect.
3. The counseling activities are an ordinary and regular part of the religious counselor's duties.
4. The religious counselor does not use or imply the use of regulated professional titles unless licensed to do so.

The New Jersey statute (1978) exempting "members of other professional groups doing work of psychological nature" from licensure states:

> Nothing in this act shall be construed to prevent qualified members of other professional groups such as physicians, osteopaths, optometrists, chiropractors, *members of the clergy, authorized practitioners,* attorneys at law, social workers or guidance counselors from doing work of a psychological nature consistent with the accepted standards of their respective professions, provided, however, that they do not hold themselves out to the public by any title or description stating or implying that they are psychologists or are licensed to practice psychology. (Emphasis added.)

Unordained or unlicensed seminary students probably do not qualify for the exemption. Therefore, seminary students should not hold themselves out as counselors but rather as pastoral care trainees or other such designation. Lay readers, Christian education directors, and other church workers without ordination or licensure as "clergy" also do not qualify. Generally, "authorized practitioners" refers to Christian Science practitioners who are registered by that denomination to perform certain healing tasks.

There is no limiting language on what religious groups or sects qualify for the exemption. This inclusive reading is in keeping with broad First Amendment prohibitions against favoring one religious group over another. For example, the law cannot allow ordained clergy from the Roman Catholic Church to take advantage of the exemption while excluding an Imam from the local Moslem mosque.

Although not explicit in the New Jersey statute, many states expressly note that the clergy must be under the authority of their respective denominations. The denomination or sect must have the authority to set standards for its clergy and to apply disciplinary procedures when those standards are transgressed. Denominations themselves do not universally set standards for their clergy counselors.

New Jersey's exemption applies only to those clergy who counsel within the "accepted standards of their respective professions." This element of the exemption has two parts. First, the counseling must be done under the auspices of specific job requirements. For example, if the clergy person is an administrator or legislative advocate who conducts counseling of individuals (whether for pay or not), he/she may well fall outside the exemption. Accordingly, for the religious counselor who makes a habit of counseling community members outside of the congregation, the exemption seems less likely.

Second, the counseling must fall within the expectations of the cleric's denominational standards. This can be somewhat vague, especially where the denomination has no written standards for counseling activities. However, this exemption applies specifically where the religious counselor discusses spiritual issues and considerations with his/her counselees. Although spiritual or religious issues are here defined broadly, the religious counselor should avoid strictly psychiatric diagnoses and interventions.

Religious counselors can always refer congregants or clients suffering from psychiatric disorders to mental health professionals, and serious consideration should be given to this option. However, there is no guarantee that congregants or clients will heed such suggestions.

As previously stated, the religious counselor should never express or imply that he/she possesses the titles (L.P.C., pastoral counselor, etc.) reserved by statute unless he/she is permitted to do so. Most states specify that any exemption given to religious counselors is contingent upon their not illegally using professional titles. Using a professional title is a privilege that can be earned only after the state requirements are met and the state authorizes such a use—usually by a certificate and registration number.

Whether or not one should seek state licensure is a matter of judgment. Some considerations are important here, including the interests of the religious counselor, the necessities of his/her professional duties, and the demands of his/her constituencies. The issue of whether or not clergy should be required to be licensed has been considered. At least one author has concluded that, although the First Amendment probably shields the clergy from state-required licensing, the public is most protected by establishing licensing requirements for religious counselors, including minimum competency in assessment, treatment, and referral. (Troyer, 1989).

Criminal Sanctions Related to Licensure

Every state imposes criminal sanctions for violation of the state licensing requirements. These sanctions generally cover two types of infractions. The first infraction involves the improper use of professional titles or descriptions of professional counseling services. The second type of infraction involves professional misconduct.

Regarding the unlawful use of a professional title or description of services, South Carolina's statute (1986) typifies such laws:

> It is unlawful for any person who is not licensed in the manner prescribed in this chapter to represent himself as a licensed professional counselor, licensed associate counselor, or licensed marital or family therapist or to hold himself out to the public as being licensed under this chapter by means of using a title on signs, mailboxes, address plates, stationery, announcements, telephone listings, calling cards, or other instruments of professional identification.

Regarding the improper description of professional counseling services, many states make it illegal to describe counseling services in terms that are likely to confuse the public. All states define "counseling" in their licensing statutes. Vermont (1989) defines "clinical mental health counseling" as

> providing professional services based on psychotherapeutic techniques and theories, including consulting and referral, to assist individuals and groups in developing an understanding of personal and interpersonal problems, defining goals, making decisions, planning courses of action reflecting personal needs, interests, and abilities, and using informational and community resources to achieve optimal mental health and effective personal, social, educational and vocational development and adjustment.

The difference between counseling and religious counseling is the spiritual elements and goals of the latter. Thus, advertising must emphasize the spiritual dimensions of the religious counseling.

The South Carolina statute makes the unlawful use of a professional title a misdemeanor with a fine not to exceed $100. Most states set the penalty between $500 and $1000; some states allow the judge to impose a jail term as well. Additionally, most states require that applicants have not previously broken any of the regulations.

Sanctions are also imposed for misconduct. These sanctions are usually administrative in nature (not criminal), and the offending acts, as well as possible sanctions, are stated in the statute. Florida law (1991) provides an example of the prohibited conduct:

(a) Attempting to obtain a counseling license by fraud or misrepresentation.

. . . .

(c) Being convicted or found guilty of a crime directly relating to counseling.

(d) False or deceptive advertising or obtaining a fee on the representation that beneficial results from any treatment will be guaranteed.

. . . .

(f) Maintaining a professional relationship with anyone whom the licensee knows, or has reason to believe, is in violation of licensing laws.

(g) Knowingly aiding, procuring, or advising a nonlicensed person to hold himself out as licensed or certified.

. . . .

(j) Paying or receiving a kickback, rebate, or bonus for receiving or referring a counselee.

(k) Committing any act upon a counselee which would constitute sexual battery or sexual misconduct.

. . . .

Florida also details its sanctions; these include one or more of the following: denial of a license to those unlicensed persons who violate the laws, temporary or permanent revocation of a license, suspension of a license for up to five years, imposition of an administrative fine not to exceed $1,000 for each count, public reprimand, probation, and/or restriction of practice.

Arguments Against Counseling Licensure

There are at least two reasons *not* to pursue licensure. Religious counselors do not need licensure to conduct counseling within the parameters of their congregation. So long as religious counselors do not represent themselves as possessing counseling credentials they do not have, most states specify that their licensing laws do not apply to religious counselors.

Second, licensure carries with it additional responsibilities. Such duties include the full range of assessment, intervention techniques, and legal and ethical considerations (abuse reporting) imposed upon any secular counselor. Licensure is a double-edged sword.

Conclusion: Practice Pointers

The following practice tips and pointers arise from the legal considerations of this chapter. These suggestions may be useful as guidelines; however, each case presents unique facts.

1. The exemption for clergy and other religious counselors is predicated partly upon the counseling requirements in the "usual course" of employment. Religious counselors should have a written, updated, and accurate job description for their positions. This is particularly true where counseling is not indicated in the job description, but is a part of the work requirements.

2. Religious counselors must be very careful not to use titles or a description of their counseling services that might mislead the public as to counseling licensure. Using the term "pastoral counselor," "licensed counselor," or "pastoral counseling" on business cards or letterhead, contrary to state statute, can easily mislead the public. Verbal or written descriptions of counseling services that go beyond the job requirements (e.g., premarital counseling, bereavement counseling, or spiritual advice) may both misrepresent the competency of the counseling offered and stray from the exempted counseling functions of the religious counselor.

3. Should counseling either be a significant part of a religious counselor's role or become a significant part, serious consideration should be given to becoming licensed by the state. First, state licensure is a fundamental way that counselors become minimally qualified to render competent counseling. Second, licensure will ensure that the religious counselor does not extend his or her counseling services beyond the legal mandates of the religious exemptions.

4. Those religious counselors working in states without exemptions for their counseling activities should not despair. The First Amendment will protect clearly spiritual and religious counseling that is authorized by the denomination, sect, or religious certifying body. However, particularly for these religious counselors, documents describing how the religious certifying body views the role of counseling are imperative. Additionally, these religious counselors should possess an accurate, current job description specifically detailing the amount of counseling and the type of counseling the position requires.

5. If religious counselors decide to become licensed in counseling, they should follow the state regulations closely. They could approach

the licensing board as to whether their theological degree will constitute the requisite master's counseling degree and whether clinical chaplaincies constitute the requisite supervised experience.

References

California (BPC), Title 13, § 4980 (1990).

Delaware statute, Title 24, § 3001 (1987).

Family Counseling Serv. v. Rust, 462 F. Supp. 74 (D. Nev. 1978).

Florida statute, § 491.009(2) (1991).

Magleby v. State, 564 P.2d 1109 (Utah, 1977).

Maine statute, 32 § 13851 (7-A) (1990).

New Jersey statute, § 45:14 B-A (1978).

South Carolina statute, § 40-75-70 (1986 & Supp. 1990).

State v. Melvin, 132 N.H. 308, 564 A.2d 458 (1989).

Troyer, R. C. (1989). Protecting the Flock from the Shepherd: A Duty of Care and Licensing Requirements for Clergy Counselors. *Boston College Law Review, 30*, 1179–1220.

Vermont statute, Title 26, § 3261(1) (1989).

Table 4.1
State Licensing Codes for Selected Counseling Professions, Including Pastoral Counselors

Legend: LPC = Licensed Professional Counselor; M & FC (or FT) = Marriage and Family Counselor (or Family Therapist); LP = Licensed Psychologist; PC = Professional Counselor; Past. C = Pastoral Counselor; CC = Certified Counselor; M, F, & CC = Marriage, Family, and Child Counselor; LMC = Licensed Marriage Counselor; MHC= Mental Health Counselor; RPro. = Registered Professional Counselor; CPC = Certified Professional Counselor; LMHC = Licensed Mental Health Counselor; RPract. = Registered Practicing Counselor; SW = Social Worker; LSW = Licensed Social Worker; CMH = Counselor in Mental Health; CSW = Certified Social Worker; MC = Marriage Counselor; MM = Marital Mediator; Cl.MHC = Clinical Mental Health Counselor; CMHC = Certified Mental Health Counselor.

State	Code	Profession	Educational Requirements
Alabama (1985)	34-8A-1ff.	LPC	30 graduate hours in counseling
Alaska (1990)	08.86.180	LP	
Arizona (Supp. 1990)	32-3311	M & FC	Master's/Doctorate in various disciplines
	32-3301	CC	Master's degree in counseling
Arkansas (1987)	17-24-101	LPC	Set by board
California (BPC 1990)	4980.02	M, F, & CC	Master's degree
Colorado (1990)	12-43-601	LPC	Master's/Doctorate in counseling
Connecticut (1989)	20-195a	M & FT	Master's degree in pastoral counseling
Delaware (1987)	3001	PC	Master's degree "primarily" in counseling
District of Columbia (1988)	2-3308ff.	SW	(various categories of social worker) Bachelor's or Master's degree, depending upon certification

State	Code	Profession	Educational Requirements
Florida (Supp. 1991)	491.005(4)	MHC	Master's degree "related" to mental health counseling
Georgia (Supp. 1990)	43-10A-3ff.	PC	Master's degree "primarily" in counseling
Hawaii (Supp. 1990)	467Dff.	SW	Master's degree in social work
Idaho (1988)	54-3401ff.	LPC	Planned Master's degree "primarily" in counseling
Illinois (1990)	Ch. 111, 6351	SW	Master's degree in social work
Indiana (1991)	25-23.6, ch. 7	M & FC	Master's degree in marriage or family or in "related" area
Iowa (1989)	154C.1ff.	SW	Master's degree in social work
Kansas (Supp. 1989)	65-5801ff.	RPro.	60 graduate semester hours and graduate degree in counseling with specific course content
Kentucky (Supp. 1990)	335.080ff.	SW	Bachelor's degree in social work
Louisiana (1988 & Supp. 1991)	37:1104	LPC	48 graduate semester hours and graduate degree that is mental health in content, with specific course content
Maine (Supp. 1990)	32, 13851	Past. C.	Set by state board
Maryland (1991)	17-101	CPC	Master's degree in a counseling field
Massachusetts (Supp. 1990)	112, 165	LMHC	Master's degree in "relevant" field
Michigan (Supp. 1990)	333. 18101	LPC	Master's degree in counseling or student personnel work
		MC	Master's degree in pastoral counseling
Minnesota (1989 & Supp. 1991)	148B.40	M & FT	Master's degree in marriage and family therapy

Continued on next page

State	Code	Profession	Educational Requirements
Mississippi (1989)	73-30-1	LPC	60 semester hours with educational specialist's degree or degree related to counseling
Missouri (Supp. 1991)	337.500	LPC	Master's degree with major or specialization in counseling
Montana (1989)	37-23-101ff.	LPC	Planned graduate degree "primarily" in counseling
Nebraska (Supp. 1987)	71-1,267ff.	CPC	Established by board
Nevada (1991)	641A.010	M & FT	Graduate degree in marriage and family therapy, social work, or psychology
New Hampshire (Supp. 1990)	330A:16-c	Past. C.	Master's degree from theological school plus Master's/Doctorate in counseling
	328-C:4	MM	Program of instruction
New Jersey (1990)	45:8B-1	LMC	Master's degree in pastoral counseling
New Mexico (Supp. 1989)	61-31-3	SW	(various) Bachelor's degree in social work
New York (1990)	Education Law 7603	LP	Doctorate in psychology or equivalent
	Education Law 7701	CSW	Master's degree in social work or equivalent
North Carolina (1990)	90-329ff.	RPract.	Master's degree including a concentration in subject matter directly related to practice of counseling
North Dakota (Supp. 1989)	43-47-01ff.	LPC	Master's degree meeting board requirements
Ohio (1987 & Supp. 1990)	4757.01ff.	PC	Master's degree in counseling, with 60 quarter hours of counselor training

State	Code	Profession	Educational Requirements
Oklahoma (1989)	59, 1901	LPC	Master's degree with 45 semester hours "concentrating" in some counseling area
(Supp. 1991)	59, 1925.1	M & F T	Master's degree with 36 hours "primarily" in family therapy
Oregon (Supp. 1990)	675.705	LPC	Graduate degree in counseling
Pennsylvania (Supp. 1990)	63, 1901	LSW	Master's degree in social work
Puerto Rico (1988)	20, 821	SW	Bachelor's degree in social work and experience
Rhode Island (1987 & Supp. 1990)	5-63-2	CMH	60 semester hours with graduate degree "specializing" in counseling/therapy
		M & FT	60 semester hours with graduate degree "specializing" in marital and family therapy
South Carolina (1986 & Supp. 1990)	40-75-80ff.	LPC	Master's degree "primarily" in counseling
		M & FT	Master's degree "primarily" in marital and family therapy
South Dakota (Supp. 1990)		LPC	Master's degree "primarily" in counseling
Tennessee (1990)	63-22-101ff.	LPC	60 graduate semester hours with major in counseling
		M & FT	Compatible with AAFT national standards
Texas (Supp. 1991)	71, 4512gff.	LPC	Master's degree with 30 graduate hours in counseling
Utah (1990)	58-39-1ff.	M & FT	Graduate degree in field of religious study that includes instruction and supervision in marriage and family therapy
Vermont (Supp. 1990)	26, 3261	CMHC	Master's degree in mental health counseling or allied health field
Virginia (1988)	54.1-3500	LPC Past. C.	Established by board Requirements specified by board

Continued on next page

State	Code	Profession	Educational Requirements
Virgin Islands (Supp. 1990)	27, 531	SW	Master's degree in social work
Washington (1989 & Supp. 1991)	18.19.010	Cl.MHC	Master's degree with 30 semester hours in mental health counseling or "substantial equivalent"
West Virginia (1986)	30-31-1	LPC	Master's degree in "closely related" counseling field
Wisconsin (1988 & Supp. 1990)	455.01	Psychology	Doctoral degree
Wyoming (1990)	33-38-101	LPC	Master's degree in counseling or related field

Table 4.2
State Statutes Specifically Exempting Counseling Activities of Professionals, Including Religious Counselors

State	Code	Exemption and Specifications
Alaska	08.86.185(5)(d)	Clinical Social Worker
Arizona	32-3271(4)	Rabbi, Priest, or other Clergy acting within scope of employment in legally recognized church, denomination, or sect
Arkansas	17-24-103	Clergy, Listed Christian Scientist Practitioners
California (BPC 1990)	4980.01	This chapter shall not apply to any priest, rabbi, or minister of the gospel of any religious denomination when performing counseling services as part of his or her pastoral or professional duties.
Connecticut	20-195q	Social work services for "recognized educational institution, a federal, state, or municipal institution, a community action agency"
Delaware	Ch. 24 Section 3002(5)(a) and Section 3004(3)	"religious counseling" construing "religious activity" as: "in the broadest sense possible to include all activity: a. Arguably protected by either the free exercise or the establishment clauses of the First Amendment to the United States Constitution; b. Arguably protected by Sect. 1, article 1 of the Constitution of this state; c. Which can be shown to have been historically engaged in by any religiously motivated person or legal entity; or d. Which can be shown is sincerely believed to be described in, or mandated by, the Holy Scriptures of the individual or legal entity involved. Religious activity is not limited in any way to Sabbath worship but extends to any activity of a spiritual or religious nature which touches in any way on the affairs of life. Religious activity is not limited to clergy or churches and it includes church members or other religiously motivated individuals"

Continued on next page

State	Code	Exemption and Specifications
Georgia (Supp. 1990)	43-10A-7	(7) Active members of the clergy but only when the practice of their specialty is in the course of their service as clergy; (8) Members of religious ministries responsible to their established ecclesiastical authority who possess a master's degree or its equivalent in theological studies; (9) Persons engaged in the practice of a specialty in accordance with Biblical doctrine in public or nonprofit agencies or entities or in private practice
Hawaii (Supp. 1990)	467D-8	(3) Any minister, priest, rabbi, or officer of any religious denomination who has been ordained or is authorized to perform official acts according to the practices of such denomination
Idaho (1988)	54-3402	Exempt so long as person does not hold self out as "licensed counselor"
Illinois (1990)	6354(4)	2. Nothing in this Act shall be construed to apply to any person engaged in the bona fide practice of religious ministry provided the person does not hold himself out to be engaged in the independent practice of clinical social work or the practice of social work.
Indiana (1991)	25-23.6(2)	(a) This article may not be construed to limit the services performed by a person who does not use a title specified in this article and who is: (4) a rabbi, priest, Christian Science practitioner, minister, or other member of the clergy; (5) an employee of or a volunteer for a nonprofit corporation or an organization performing charitable, religious, or educational functions, providing pastoral counseling or other assistance
Louisiana (1988)	13, 1113	(8) Any priest, rabbi, Christian Science practitioner, or minister of the gospel of any religious denomination
Maine (Supp. 1990)	32, 13856	2. Nothing in this chapter may be construed to apply to the activities and services of any priest, rabbi, clergyman, including a

State	Code	Exemption and Specifications
		Christian Science healer, or minister of the gospel of any religious denomination when performing counseling services as part of religious duties and in connection with a specific synagogue or church of any religious denomination.
Maryland (1991)	17-103	Other health practitioners
Massachusetts (Supp. 1990)	112, 164	(4) Nothing in this chapter shall be construed to prevent qualified members of other professions including Christian Science practitioners, registered nurses, physicians, attorneys, or members of the clergy from doing the work of an allied mental health and human services professional consistent with the accepted standards of their respective professions; provided, however, that no such person shall use a title stating or implying that they are a licensed allied mental health and human services professional.
Michigan (Supp. 1990)	333. 18115(2)	(a) An ordained member of the clergy if counseling is incidental to his or her religious duties performed under the auspices or recognition of a church, denomination, religious association, or sect [pursuant to the tax code] if the member of the clergy does not hold him or herself out as a counselor licensed under this code.
		(b) An individual who performs volunteer services for a public or private nonprofit organization, church, or charity, if the individual is approved by the organization or agency for which the services are rendered.
(Supp. 1990)	339.1504	This article shall not apply to an ordained cleric or other religious practitioner recognized by the department if the advice or counsel is incidental to duties as a cleric or other religious practitioner, and if the cleric or other religious practitioner does not advertise as a marriage counselor.

Continued on next page

State	Code	Exemption and Specifications
Minnesota (1989)	148B.38	Nothing in this [law] shall be construed to prevent qualified members of other . . . occupations, such as . . . members of the clergy . . . while performing those duties for which they are employed . . . from doing work of a marriage counselor
Mississippi (1989)	73-30-25	It is not the intent of this chapter to regulate against members of other duly regulated professions in this state who do counseling in the normal course of the practice of their own profession. This chapter does not apply to: (h) Duly ordained ministers or clergy while functioning in their ministerial capacity and duly accredited Christian Science practitioners
Missouri (Supp. 1991)	337.505	[These laws] do not apply to: (6) Duly ordained ministers or clergy or religious workers while functioning in their ministerial capacity; . . . (9) Duly accredited Christian Science practitioners, so long as they are practicing within the scope of Christian Science principles
Nebraska (Supp. 1987)	71-1,256	Nothing in [these laws] shall be construed to prevent: (1) Qualified members of other professions, including . . . members of the clergy . . . from doing work consistent with the scope of practice of their respective professions, except that such qualified members shall not hold themselves out to the public by title as being engaged in the practice of social work
Nevada (1991)	641A.410	2. The provisions of this chapter do not: (d) Apply to a licensed or ordained minister in good standing with his denomination whose duty is primarily to serve his congregation and whose practice of marriage and family therapy is incidental to his other duties if he does not hold himself out to the public by any title or description

State	Code	Exemption and Specifications
		of service that is likely to cause confusion with the titles and descriptions or services set forth in this chapter
New Jersey (1978)	45:14B-8	Clergy and "authorized practitioners" working within "the accepted standards of their respective professions" provided they do not hold themselves out as psychologists
New Mexico (Supp. 1989)	61-31-5	Exempts other recognized professionals from social work licensure as long as they do not represent themselves as "licensed social workers"
New York Mental Hygiene Law (1989)	31.02(a)(3)(iii)	Exemption to resident facilities from operating certificate for "pastoral counseling by a clergyman or minister including those defined as clergyman or minister"
(1985)	Art. 7605 Education Law	Exempts classes of psychologists
North Carolina (1990)	90-330	(b) Nothing in this article shall be construed as authorizing Registered Practicing Counselors to engage in the practice of law, and such person shall not engage in the practice of law unless duly licensed so to do.
North Dakota (Supp. 1989)	43-47-04	(5) This chapter does not prevent a member of the clergy of any denomination from providing services within the scope of ministerial services
		(6) This chapter does not prevent the employment of, or volunteering by, individuals in nonprofit agencies or community organizations if these persons do not hold themselves out to the public as professional counselors or associate counselors
Ohio (Supp. 1990)	4759.16	This section shall not apply to. . . (D) Rabbis, priests, Christian Science practitioners, clergy, or members of religious orders and other individuals participating with them in pastoral counseling when the counseling

Continued on next page

State	Code	Exemption and Specifications
		activities are within the scope of the performance of their regular duties and are performed under the auspices or sponsorship of an established and legally cognizable church, denomination, or sect or an integrated auxiliary of a church . . . and when the individual rendering the service remains accountable to the established authority of that church, denomination, sect, or integrated auxiliary.
Oklahoma (Supp. 1991)	59, 1925.3	B. The Marital and Family Therapist Licensure Act Shall not be construed to apply to the professional pursuit of qualified members of other professional groups, including but limited to. . . members of the clergy who are in good standing with their denominations, Christian Science practitioners, lay pastoral counselors . . . Provided, however, no such person shall use a title or description stating or implying that such a person is a licensed marital or family therapist.
(1989)	59, 1903	The Licensed Professional Counselors Act shall not be construed to include the professional pursuits of clergymen, lay pastoral counselors, . . . insofar as such activities and services are a part of the official duties in salaried positions and the title "licensed professional counselor" or "LPC" is not used.
Pennsylvania (Supp. 1990)	63, 1902	This act regulates only those who hold themselves out as licensed social workers.
Rhode Island (Supp. 1990)	5-63-11	(2) No person shall be required to be certified under this chapter who:
		(d) is a rabbi, priest, minister, or member of the clergy of any religious denomination or sect when engaging in activities which are within the scope of the performance of his or her regular or specialized ministerial duties and for which no separate charge is made, or when such activities are performed, with or without charge, for or under the auspices or sponsorship, individually or in conjunction with others, of an established and legally cognizable

State	Code	Exemption and Specifications
		church, denomination, or sect, and when the person rendering service remains accountable to the established authority thereof
South Carolina (1986 & Supp. 1990)	40-75-190	Individuals in the following classifications who are performing services of a nature consistent with their training and which services are similar to those described in this chapter are exempt from the provisions of this chapter so long as they do not represent themselves by a title or description in the manner described [above]:
		(5) Any rabbi, clergyman, or person of similar status who is a member in good standing of, and accountable to, a recognized denomination or religious organization and who is exercising ministerial responsibilities in the religious body, parish, church ministry, or institutional ministry with which he is associated
Tennessee (1990)	63-22-113	Other licensed counselors
Texas (Supp. 1991)	71, 4512g 3.	(4) the activities and services of licensed members of other professions, such as . . . Christian Science practitioners who are recognized religious practitioners performing counseling consistent with the law of the state, their training, and any code of ethics of their professions, if they do not represent themselves by any title or description
		(6) the activities, services, titles, and descriptions of persons employed as professionals or as volunteers in the practice of counseling for public and private nonprofit organizations or charities
Utah (1990)	58-39-5	The following persons who do marriage and family therapy as part of their professional practice and within the discipline of their profession shall not be required to be licensed under this chapter:

Continued on next page

State	Code	Exemption and Specifications
		(2) any priest, rabbi, clergyman, or minister of the gospel of any religious denomination, when performing counseling services as a part of his religious duties and in connection with a specific church or synagogue of any religious denomination.
Virginia (1988)	54.1-3501	The requirements for licensure in this chapter shall not be applicable to:
		3. The activities of rabbis, priests, ministers or clergymen of any denomination or sect when such activities are within the scope of the performance of their regular or specialized ministerial duties, and no separate charge is made or when such activities are performed, whether with or without charge, for or under auspices or sponsorship, individually or in conjunction with others, of an established and legally cognizable church, denomination, or sect and the person rendering the service remains accountable to its established authority.
Virgin Islands (Supp. 1990)	27, 533	(b) Nothing in this chapter shall be construed to prevent licensed . . . members of the clergy from doing work within the standards and ethics of their respective professions and callings, provided they do not hold themselves out to the public by title or description of service as being engaged in the practice of social work.
Washington (1989)	18.19.040	Nothing in this chapter may be construed to prohibit or restrict:
		(6) The practice of counseling by a person under the auspices of a religious denomination, church, or organization, or the practice of religion itself
West Virginia (1986)	30-31-3	(a) Nothing in this article applies to the following activities:
		(7) The activities and services of qualified members of other recognized professions such as . . . clergymen performing counseling consistent with the laws of this state, their training and any code of ethics of their professions so long as such persons do not represent themselves as licensed professional counselors

State	Code	Exemption and Specifications
Wisconsin (1988)	455.02(2)	Other psychological services
	448.03	(g) Ritual circumcision by a rabbi is exempted from licensure for surgery
	448.03(6)	No law in this state regulating the practice of medicine and surgery may be construed to interfere with the practice of Christian Science. A person who elects Christian Science treatment in lieu of medical or surgical treatment for the cure of disease may not be compelled to submit to medical or surgical treatment.
Wyoming (1990)	33-38-103	(b) This act does not apply to:
		(ii) Religious leaders and practitioners pursuing their primary church or religious duties

5
PRIVILEGED COMMUNICATION
FOR RELIGIOUS COUNSELORS

[I]t is necessary to desist from this custom . . . lest many be put off from availing themselves of the remedies of penance, either through shame or through fear of seeing revealed to their enemies deeds for which they may be subject to the action of the law. . . . Only then will many allow themselves to be summoned to penance, if the conscience of him who is confessing is not to be revealed to the ears of the people.
—*Pope Leo I*

A Case Study

The following real-life case illustrates the concept of privileged communication. Helen was married to Malcolm for many years but was recently granted a divorce. One month after the divorce, Malcolm married Loretta. Helen sued Loretta in a South Carolina state court for "alienation of affections." Loretta admitted having sexual intercourse with Malcolm prior to his divorce. A jury found that Loretta had intentionally disturbed the relationship between Malcolm and Helen and awarded Helen $70,000.

As part of the appeal, Loretta argued that the minister—acting as Helen's personal counselor—should be forced to testify. The minister-counselor provided psychotherapy under the auspices of a local Methodist church. Loretta asserted that the minister's testimony would substantiate her claim that she did not destroy Helen's marriage. The minister protested that he should not be required to divulge private, therapeutic conversations.

Several factors are important. First, the minister's testimony would help to ascertain the truth or falsity of the allegations. However, ministers enjoy a privilege from forced testimony as do other professionals. For example, lawyers do not have to testify against their clients, and normally a person does not have to testify against his/her spouse. As a matter of public policy and personal expectations, Helen's private counseling sessions should not be exposed in open court. She entered into counseling relying on the assumption that her conversations would be kept confidential. Religious counseling or confession would not be therapeutic if disclosures were subject to public testimony.

Interpreting Privileged Communication Law: The Case of Loretta and Malcom

The court began its discussion by examining the applicable South Carolina clergy privileged communication statute. Statute § 19-11-90 (1976) reads in part:

> no regular or duly ordained minister, priest, or rabbi shall be required, in giving testimony, to disclose any confidential communication properly entrusted to him in his professional capacity and necessary and proper to enable the clergyman to discharge the functions of his office according to the usual course of practice or discipline

The court determined that the minister was an ordained minister and that Helen intended her therapy sessions with him to be confidential. The real issues were (1) whether the minister acted in the professional capacity of a counselor or of a minister and (2) whether the communications were "necessary and proper" to discharge his functions.

First, the court found that marital issues in therapy often involve religious or spiritual issues. Then the court considered the fact that a local Methodist church sponsored the minister's counseling activities. Although the court noted the difficulty in determining whether the minister was acting more as a counselor or as a clergy person, the court concluded that the minister was acting in his ministerial capacity.

Second, the court concluded that confidential communications were necessary for the minister to carry out his functions as a clergy person. In making this determination, the court reemphasized the fact that marriage counseling is a regular part of a clergyperson's job. Given the court's conclusions, it ruled that the privilege would be honored and that the minister could not be forced to testify in court on the substance of his counseling sessions with Helen. (*Rivers v. Rivers*, 1987).

Clergy Privileged Communication Defined

"Privileged communication" refers to an immunity granted to certain people and professionals that exempts them from testifying in court. This exemption runs contrary to the usual obligation to testify in both civil and criminal cases, such obligation being necessary for credible fact finding and the rendering of justice.

A Colorado statute (§ 13–90–107[C] 1988) grants this privilege:

> A clergyman, minister, priest, or rabbi shall not be examined without both his consent and also the consent of the person asking the confidential

communication as to any confidential communication made to him in his professional capacity in the course of discipline expected by the religious body to which he belongs.

Colorado law also grants limited immunities to physicians, attorneys, surgeons, and spouses.

Granting a class of persons (professional or otherwise) a privilege that exempts them from testifying in court is not taken lightly by judges or legislatures. The common law, the body of law that flows from judicial decisions and originally emanated from English courts in early American jurisprudence, did not grant a universal clergy privilege. (*Hester v. Barnett*, 1987; *Seidman v. Fishburne-Hudgins Educ. Found.*, 1984). American courts had to recognize the privilege independently or wait until the state legislatures acted. For example, in 1855 a Virginia state court considered a deathbed confession of the wife of an accused murderer. At that time, Virginia had no privileged communication statute, and the court found no case law in America or England considering privileged communication of a Catholic priest. Because of the long-standing tradition of confessions in the Roman Catholic Church and their personal and social importance, the court held that the priest would enjoy the privilege and could not be called as a witness. (*Commonwealth v. Cronin*, 1855). Generally, judges prefer to interpret statutory law rather than to create laws on their own initiative.

The California legislature has statutorily created the clergy privilege, reasoning that it did not want to compel clergy to violate—nor to punish clergy for refusing to violate—the tenets of their religious doctrine where confidentiality is required of them. Additionally, in California (and some other states) the clergy person is not obligated to abide by the privilege. Therefore, the clergy person may testify if he/she wishes to if the penitent fails to assert the privilege or is deceased, legally incompetent, or absent. Conversely, some states require the clergy to abide by the privilege no matter what, even if the counselee waives the privilege. In other instances, if the counselee has stated that he/she does not care if the pastor discloses the contents of the counseling session, the religious counselor must testify. Finally, in some states, the counselee cannot waive the privilege even if he/she wants to. It is important to note that the pastor's duties under the law are governed by the state where the pastor is called to testify.

Elements Necessary to Invoke the Privilege

Today, all of the states and some American protectorates have passed clergy privileged communication laws. These laws specifically define who can invoke the privilege and under what circumstances the privilege will be recognized. Table 5.1 lists the statute citation for each state. Table 5.1 also specifies some of the qualifications necessary to claim the privilege. Note that some qualifications use terms of art such as "in professional character or capacity." This term refers to the clergy person's professional function and is defined below. Each statute contains specific elements that must be satisfied before the privilege will be effective. Generally, these are (1) the religious counselor has maintained a professional identity as "clergy"; (2) the confessor has manifested a confidential intent; (3) the clergy person is acting in his or her professional capacity; (4) no one has waived the privilege; and (5) other laws do not require the testimony.

Professional Identity as Clergy

All of the clergy privileged communication statutes specify that the one confided in must be professionally identified as a "clergy person" or other religious or spiritual leader. Alabama (§ 12-21-166[a], 1986) defines "clergy" as

> [a]ny duly ordained, licensed, or commissioned minister, pastor, priest, rabbi or practitioner of any bona fide established church or religious organization and shall include and be limited to any person who regularly, as a vocation, devotes a substantial portion of his time and abilities to the service of his respective church or religious organization.

Connecticut (§ 52-146b, 1989) assigns the privilege to "[a] clergyman, priest, minister, rabbi or practitioner of any religious denomination accredited by the religious body to which he belongs who is settled in the work of the ministry."

Courts and legislatures generally try to define "religion" very broadly, not wanting to exclude people with sincere beliefs. Although privileged communication laws seek to be religiously inclusive, they tend to be very exacting when defining "clergy person."

A New Jersey court had to decide whether a Roman Catholic nun should be considered "clergy" for the purpose of claiming privileged communication. (*In re Murtha*, 1971). Sister Margaret, a member of the Dominican sisterhood (a teaching order), was awakened at her convent when one of her students, suspected of murder, wanted to speak with her. A grand jury asked Sister Margaret a series of questions relating to the suspect's alleged confession to her. She refused to answer, claiming a clergy privilege. The state, wanting the court to disallow the privilege, argued that (1) a priest's duties in the Roman Catholic Church are dissimilar to those of a nun; (2) priests and nuns have separate functions;

(3) Sister Margaret's superiors urged her to testify; and (4) nothing in Roman Catholic doctrine would support her claim. Accordingly, the court placed her in jail for refusing to testify.

Whether Presbyterian elders are "clergy" for the purposes of privileged communication statutes was considered by the Supreme Court of Iowa. A father claimed his minor daughter had sexual intercourse with the defendant. The daughter, fourteen and pregnant, confessed before the church Session (current "elders"). The defendant, wanting the elders to testify, claimed that the girl's confession before the Session would show that he was not the only man in the girl's life and that the paternity of the child was open to question. The girl's father, arguing against the elders' testimony, claimed that the confession should not be made public because it was a privileged communication between the penitent and her "clergy."

In making its decision, the court examined church documents containing the rule and policy of the Presbyterian church. The court found that in Presbyterian church polity, elders are considered "ministers of the gospel," that their duties include "spiritual government of the congregation," and that elders may lead Session meetings under certain conditions. The court ruled that pursuant to Presbyterian doctrine, elders are considered ministers and as such the girl's confession was entitled to the clergy privilege of confidentiality. (*Reutkemeier v. Nolte*, 1917).

The Confessor's Confidential Intent

For the privilege to be recognized, the one confessing (the penitent) to the clergy must expect his or her confession to be held in confidence. Hawaii (Rules of Evidence 506, 1985) protects statements that are "made privately and not intended for further disclosure except to other persons present in furtherance of the purpose of the communication."

In one interesting case, Bottoson, arrested for murder, confessed his crime to a minister who was visiting the Florida prison where Bottoson was held before trial. Bottoson was convicted on the testimony that the minister was forced to disclose. The appellate court found that Bottoson's cell-mate advised him to confess to a minister so that the minister would relay the information to the office of the state's attorney. The court held that because Bottoson's confessions were intended to be divulged to a third party (the state's attorney), the statements were not privileged. (*Bottoson v. State*, 1983).

In a case related to the concept of confession, a woman died, and her will was contested by her son. He alleged that his mother was the victim of undue influence. A minister had regularly visited and counseled the woman while she was in a nursing home. The court determined that the minister's testimony regarding the woman's mental competency during the time that she made her will would not be related to a confession or admission. The religious counselor's testimony was available to the court. (*Buuck v. Kruckeberg*, 1950).

Professional Capacity

After a court determines that the religious counselor is a "clergy person" within the meaning of the privileged communication statute and that the confessor intended the communication to be private, the court must determine that the clergy was acting in his or her professional capacity as a clergy person or other religious leader.

Professional Capacity in Criminal Cases

Defendant Patterson, convicted of murder, claimed that his minister should not have been forced to testify at trial. Patterson attended the minister's church, even though he was not an active member. The minister was appointed by the court to counsel the defendant in jail on an unrelated charge of indecent exposure.

Patterson confessed the murder to his minister. The Pennsylvania clergy privileged communication statute states that the privilege applies to a clergy person "who while in the course of his duties" has acquired confidential information.

The judges found that it was the minister who approached the defendant (not the penitent who approached the minister) when the minister concluded from a newspaper article that his counselee might have been the murderer. The court found further that the defendant's communication had not been motivated by a desire for forgiveness or other religious goals. Thus, the court concluded that the minister's role was similar to that of any secular counselor and therefore he could be forced to testify. (*Commonwealth v. Patterson*, 1990).

Professional Capacity in Civil Cases

In one Georgia case (*Jones v. Department of Human Resources*, 1983), two parents, one diagnosed as a chronic schizophrenic and the other suffering from a brain injury, sued to retain custody of their four-year-old son. Because of these mental conditions, the parents were unable adequately to care for their son for periods of time, and the son was periodically placed in foster care. These parents gave voluntary custody of their son to their pastor and his wife during a two-month period. The parents lost their parental rights to their son. They based their defense partly upon their contention that because of the privileged communication statute, the pastor should not be allowed to testify as to the son's behavior.

The court had to decide whether the pastor's observations of the child could be considered communications in his professional capacity. The court held that they were not. The court found that the observations were not consistent with "spiritual counseling" or "profession of religious faith." Rather, the pastor's observations revolved around the child's condition and the child's relationship to his biological parents.

Courts will examine the nature of the communications carefully. Those claiming the privilege will need to prove more than that their conversations involved a bona fide member of the clergy and that the conversation was intended to be confidential. Those claiming the privilege will also have to prove that the communications were made in the course of the clergy's normal and regular professional duties. This means that the penitent would need to show that the communications had specific, relevant spiritual content and that the clergy person was conducting his or her activities within the norms of his or her own particular denomination or group. Although it is not necessary that a penitent "confess" within a confessional to effect the privilege, the content of the communication must be specifically directed toward spiritual goals recognized by the clergy's religious body.

Waiving the Privilege

The one who claims the privilege cannot do or say anything that is inconsistent with the expectation that the communications were intended as confidential. The following case arises from the criminal activity of a church treasurer. A woman responsible for a church fund to other charities admitted to her Episcopalian priest that she had embezzled $30,000 from the fund. She had secured loans to replace the almost-depleted funds, but the loans would not become available soon enough to cover checks already issued against the account. She told the priest that she was calling him for his help in solving the problem.

The priest responded that he was leaving town the next day, and he could either keep her secret until he returned or call upon other leaders within the church (wardens) to help solve the situation. The woman agreed to allow other wardens to help. After hearing of the problem, the church leaders decided to inform the police, and the woman was ultimately convicted. Her appeal included the claim that her initial discussions with the priest should have been privileged communications.

The court examined the nature of the conversation. The priest testified that the woman's statements to him were for secular counseling and not "absolution" and that the woman herself agreed to have the priest divulge the information to other church leaders. Thus, the court concluded that the woman waived the clergy privilege when she allowed the priest to speak with others about her problem; thus, the court refused to grant her the clergy privilege. (*People v. Edwards*, 1988).

In some cases, documents instead of conversations will be subject to the privilege. A married couple claimed that their relationship was damaged as a result of medical malpractice by their physician. The physician in this case moved to have the records of a Roman Catholic priest, from whom the couple received marriage counseling, subpoenaed for testimony. (*Ziske v. Luskin*, 1987). The couple asserted that the priest's records should be privileged under New York law. The court relied on the case of *De'udy v. De'udy* (1985) for the proposition that a couple can waive the clergy privilege if they *both* agree to waive it. In the *De'udy* case, a husband and wife, who both sought marriage counseling separately from the same minister, both waived their privilege. As a result, the court ordered the minister to testify against his wishes.

Following this logic, the *Ziske* court ruled that where the couple placed their marriage relationship at issue in a malpractice action, they both waived the clergy privilege as to marriage counseling. Other communications, not addressing their marital relationship, would continue to be privileged. Those who publicly claim that another damaged their marriage cannot also claim that evidence surrounding their marriage relationship should be privileged. The court held that communications between the priest and the couple about the marital relationship were not privileged. Yet the court ruled that nonmarital issues disclosed in counseling would be protected under the clergy privilege.

Who Can Claim the Privilege and How It Is Raised

The right of privileged communication must be requested before a judge by one of the parties—either the clergy being asked to testify or the penitent. The judge will not raise the issue spontaneously from the bench. Once the request is made, the judge must make a ruling.

The statutes of each state expressly say who can claim the clergy privilege. Table 5.2, located at the end of this chapter, catalogues who "controls" the privilege in each of the fifty states, Puerto Rico, and the Virgin Islands. Controlling the privilege means who has the legal right to exercise the privilege. The table indicates (the "X") who can claim the privilege. Some comments are used to explain or amplify how the statutes define "penitent" or "clergy." Note that some of the laws simply state that the penitent decides whether to invoke or to waive the privilege. Some states allow the penitent's guardian, conservator, personal representative, or clergy to invoke or to waive the privilege; however, these claimants can do so only *on behalf of the penitent.*

When the intent of the clergy privilege communication statute is to provide the penitent with privacy, it follows that the penitent would have control over whether the privilege is invoked or waived. When the intent of the clergy privilege communication statute is to allow the religious counselor to maintain a duty of silence, it follows that the religious counselor should have control over whether the privilege is invoked or waived.

Some states allow either the penitent or the clergy to exercise the privilege. Other states never allow a clergy person to testify, and there is no right of waiver by the penitent. In other states, the clergy person must testify if the penitent waives the privilege. In this sense, the term "clergy privilege" is something of a misnomer in that the religious counselor does not always have the statutory right to invoke or waive the privilege.

The Colorado privilege statute (§ 52-146b, 1989) provides the penitent with exclusive control:

> A clergyman, priest, minister, rabbi or practitioner of any religious denomination . . . shall not disclose confidential information . . . *unless the person making the confidential communication waives such a privilege.* (Emphasis added.)

The clergy cannot claim the privilege on his or her own behalf.

Delaware allows the clergy the option of invoking the privilege (Rules of Evidence 505c, 1987):

> **Who May Claim the Privilege.** The privilege may be claimed by the person, by his guardian or conservator, or by his personal representative if he is deceased. The clergyman may claim the privilege on behalf of the person. His authority so to do is presumed in the absence of evidence to the contrary.

The difference between the two statutes is that in Colorado the clergy person must keep silent unless there is a waiver by the penitent, whereas in Delaware the clergy person has the option of testifying unless another authorized person claims the privilege. The Delaware statute expressly defines who, *on behalf of the penitent,* may claim the privilege. This statute confers upon the clergy person no right to claim the privilege on his or her own behalf. The privilege is to be invoked to serve the interests of the penitent. However, the following statute clearly authorizes clergy to claim the privilege on his/her behalf.

One of the California clergy privilege communication statutes (§ 1034, 1966) states that clergy can claim the privilege:

> **Privilege of clergyman.** [A] clergyman, whether or not a party, has a privilege to refuse to disclose a penitential communication if he claims the privilege.

The twin California clergy privilege communication statute (§ 1033, 1966) states that the privilege also belongs to the penitent:

> **Privilege of penitent.** [A] penitent whether or not a party, has a privilege to refuse to disclose, and to prevent another from disclosing, a penitential communication if he claims the privilege.

California's statute authorizes the clergy to claim the clergy privilege *in their own right*. Whether or not clergy testify or remain silent is not dictated by the interests of another.

Professional Capacity and the Burden of Proof

Drelich was convicted of fatally stabbing his pregnant, twenty-three-year-old wife. Drelich appealed, claiming that his conviction was based on his disclosures to his rabbi, which were confidential and confessional in nature. The rabbi claimed, however, that Drelich used him only for help in securing an attorney and influence in negotiating a beneficial plea bargain agreement.

The court stated that Drelich had the burden of proof to show that he had a legal right to invoke the clergy privileged communication statute. Given the fact that the rabbi was used in a nonclergy function, the court ruled that Drelich failed to prove that he was entitled to invoke the privilege and thus failed to carry his burden. Accordingly, the court determined that the communications between Drelich and the rabbi were secular and that the privilege did not apply. Only those communications that Drelich could prove were made for religious purposes would be privileged (*People v. Drelich*, 1986).

The Meaning of the Term "Communications"

Generally, most of the cases cited involve *conversations* with religious counselors. "Communications," however, is an intentionally broad term that may protect more than the spoken word between the penitent and the clergy person. A broad interpretation may protect notes and other physical documents from being subpoenaed by the court.

In the *Patterson* (1990) case mentioned above, Patterson was linked by a toy sheriff's badge to the victim's body. Reverend Dickson was a court-appointed counselor to Patterson on unrelated arrests of indecent exposure. Dickson testified regarding Patterson's desire to confess to the murder and regarding his observations of Patterson with the badge on two occasions.

The court "categorically" rejected a privilege for openly displayed objects—such as the toy badge. All *objects* connected with a clergy communication, however, would not necessarily fall outside of the privilege. Rather, the court's ruling applied to openly displayed objects. Openly displayed objects were analogous to openly displayed conversation in that there is no intent to keep them private.

In a Massachusetts case, the court subpoenaed a Lutheran minister, Reverend Orson, to testify against defendant Miller who was charged with murder and the unlawful possession of a firearm. The prosecution asked the minister whether he saw a gun in Miller's possession. At this point, Miller's attorney requested a ruling from the bench as to whether the testimony about a gun constituted a "communication" within the meaning of the clergy privileged communication statute. The judge ruled that testimony about what the clergy *observed* could be solicited, whereas testimony about *conversation* between the clergy and the defendant could not be. Miller was convicted.

On appeal, Miller claimed that the testimony about the gun was subject to the clergy privileged communication statute and should not have been allowed. The appeals court said that the term "communications" defined in the clergy privilege statute is "not limited to conversation and includes other acts by which ideas may be transmitted from one person to another." (*Commonwealth v. Zezima*, 1974, 592). Showing a gun to a clergy person might, in some cases, constitute a privileged communication. In this case, however, the court reviewed all of the evidence produced at trial and determined that, even if Reverend Orson's testimony was omitted, Miller would have been found guilty anyway. Thus, a ruling on the privilege issue was unnecessary. Miller's appeal was denied.

Whether the notes, recordings, drawings, or other "work products" of the clergy are privileged is also a concern. If the conversation in question is privileged, then any attempt by the clergy to preserve this information should be privileged also. Many clergy keep notes or tapes from their counseling sessions as standard professional conduct.

The privilege would not, however, include paper or evidence given to the clergy by the penitent. Records of embezzlement, a murder weapon, or a victim's wallet may never be legally retained by the clergy. Nor can the clergy destroy it. Should a penitent try to leave evidence in the care of a clergy person, the clergy person should clearly advise the penitent that all clergy must turn evidence over to the authorities promptly.

The clergy, faced with the duty of loyalty to the penitent, should use all available resources to limit the information that the police will receive surrounding the evidence in question. The clergy may not wish to reveal his/her identity, and how the clergy received the evidence should be kept confidential. Clergy should not, however, alter the evidence in any way. For example, clergy should not clean, wipe, or otherwise change the evidence no matter how helpful or innocent this may seem.

The Liability of Clergy if Confidences Are Divulged

Failure of clergy to maintain confidentiality may give rise to liability. Although the clergy privileged communication law arises in both civil and criminal cases, usually divulging privileged communications does not carry criminal penalties. Normally, civil penalties can arise on a case-by-case basis as a result of lawsuits. The privilege law of Tennessee criminalizes, with possible fines and prison, clergy who are required to maintain confidences, that is, invoke the privilege, but who do not (§ 24-1-206[2][d], 1980):

> Any minister of the gospel, priest of the Catholic Church, rector of the Episcopal Church, ordained rabbi, and any regular minister of religion of any religious organization or denomination usually referred to as a church [disclosing any information communicated to him/her in a confidential manner] shall be guilty of a misdemeanor and fined not less than fifty dollars ($50.00) and imprisoned in the county jail or workhouse not exceeding six (6) months.

An important concern in this area is whether a breach of confidentiality, voluntarily or involuntarily, subjects the clergy to a tort suit independent of a statute by penitents for breach of promise, ethics, confidentiality, or other professional duty. A Missouri Court of Appeals (*Hester v. Barnett*, 1987) has ruled on this issue. Mr. and Mrs. Hester sued their minister, Reverend Barnett, for malpractice, alienation of affections, negligent counseling, and defamation.

Pastor Barnett visited the Hesters, who were not members of his church, in their home and told them that they could depend upon him to keep their confidences and that he would not divulge their private lives to others. In turn, the Hesters confided that their children had disciplinary and behavioral problems. The Hesters claimed that, contrary to Barnett's promises, he disclosed this information to church deacons, to the community, and to a child abuse hot line. The Hesters claimed that Barnett instructed the Hester children to accuse them of child abuse, as well as that Barnett disclosed falsely that Mr. Hester did not pay his employees their fair wages, that Mr. Hester was an arsonist, and that he would cheat anyone out of anything.

The court had to determine under what circumstances clergy can divulge confidential communications. The enactment of privileged communication statutes was only to promote effective communications between clergy and penitent—not to allow civil liability where such confidentiality was breached, noted the court. "[A] tenet of 'ministerial ethics' as [the Hesters allege] describes a moral, not a legal duty." The court reasoned that in the absence of any such legal duty, a moral duty cannot give rise to liability. The Missouri privileged communication statute does not provide a basis for bringing a suit against a clergy person who inappropriately breaks his/her confidences.

Nonetheless, when clergy breach confidences, stated the court, they can be sued for unreasonable intrusion upon the privacy of another or defamation or both. The *Hester* court ruled that the minister used his counseling activities as a pretense to harm the Hester family. Thus, religious counseling can be a basis for a civil suit when it is used as a pretense to harm another.

One bringing a suit for defamation must prove damage to his/her reputation resulting from false accusations of a crime, dishonesty, or other untruths likely to lower his/her esteem in the eyes of the community. The Hesters accused the minister of speaking and publishing by written word that the Hesters (1) had abused their children; (2) cheated the government; (3) stole from their neighbors; and (4) cheated their employees.

The minister in *Hester* raised the good faith immunity as a means of defending himself against the defamation charges. He claimed that his otherwise defamatory remarks should be shielded from prosecution because the Missouri child abuse reporting statute immunizes such reports. The court dismissed this assertion because the same statute denies immunities for intentionally false reports.

References

Bottoson v. State, 443 So.2d 962 (Fla. 1983), *cert. denied,* 469 U.S. 873 (1984).

Buuck v. Kruckeberg, 121 Ind. App. 262, 95 N.E.2d 304 (1950).

Commonwealth v. Cronin, 1 Quarterly Law Journal 128 (Richmond, 1855).

Commonwealth v. Patterson, 392 Pa. Super. 331, 572 A.2d 1258 (1990).

Commonwealth v. Zezima, 365 Mass. 238, 310 N.E.2d 590 (1974), *rev'd on other grounds,* 387 Mass. 748, 443 N.E.2d 1282 (1982).

De'udy v. De'udy, 130 Misc. 2d 168, 495 N.Y.S.2d 616 (1985).

Hester v. Barnett, 723 S.W.2d 544 (Mo. App. 1987).

In re Murtha, 115 N.J. Super. 380, 279 A.2d 889, *certification denied,* 59 N.J. 239, 281 A.2d 278 (1971).

Jones v. Department of Human Resources, 168 Ga. App. 915, 310 S.E.2d 753 (1983).

People v. Drelich, 123 A.2d 441, 506 N.Y.S.2d 746 (1986).

People v. Edwards, 203 Cal. App. 3d 1358, 248 Cal. Rptr. 53 (1988), *cert. denied,* 489 U.S. 1027 (1989).

Reutkemeier v. Nolte, 179 Iowa 342, 161 N.W. 290 (1917).

Rivers v. Rivers, 292 S.C. 21, 354 S.E.2d 784 (1987).

Seidman v. Fishburne-Hudgins Educ. Found., 724 F.2d 413 (4th Cir. 1984).

Ziske v. Luskin, 138 Misc. 2d 38, 524 N.Y.S.2d 145 (1987).

Table 5.1
Clergy Privileged Communication Statutes

State	Code Citation	Qualifications
Alabama	12-21-166	confession, spiritual counsel
Alaska	Rules of Court 506	
Arizona	13-4062	professional character in course of discipline
Arkansas	Rules of Court 505	confidential manner in professional character
California	Evidence Code 1030-1033	(see textual footnotes)
Colorado	13-90-107(c)	clergy cannot be examined without clergy and confessor's consent
Connecticut	52-146b	confessor must waive privilege to allow clergy to divulge
Delaware	Rules of Evidence 505	clergy may claim privilege on behalf of another
District of Columbia	14-309	"confessor, or communication" privileged
Florida	Rules of Evidence 90.505	seeking spiritual counsel in course of practice or discipline
Georgia	24-9-22	shall not disclose or cannot be compelled to disclose
Hawaii	Rules of Evidence 506	professional character as spiritual adviser
Idaho	Rules of Evidence 505	communications made privately
Illinois	Ch. 110, 8-803	in professional character as spiritual adviser
Indiana	34-1-14-5	as to confessions or admissions in course of discipline
Iowa	622.10	in professional capacity

State	Code Citation	Qualifications
Kansas	60-429	regular or duly ordained minister
Kentucky	421.210(4)	confidentially communicated in professional capacity
Louisiana	15:477	spiritual advice or consolation
Maine	Rules of Evidence 505	
Maryland	9-111	
Massachusetts	Ch. 233, 20A	no disclosure without consent of confessor
Michigan	767.5a(2)	"Any" communications privileged that enable clergy to do job
Minnesota	595.02(c)	
Mississippi	13-1-22	privilege includes clergy's secretary, stenographer and clerk
Missouri	491.060(4)	clergy legally "incompetent" to testify
Montana	26-1-804	clergy cannot divulge without consent of confessor
Nebraska	27-506	clergy may claim privilege on behalf of another
Nevada	49.255	clergy cannot testify without consent of confessor
New Hampshire	516:35	not required to disclose unless waived by confessor
New Jersey	2A:84A-23	not allowed or compelled to testify
New Mexico	11-506	clergy may claim privilege on behalf of another, in professional character
New York	Evidence Code Art. 45, 4505	professional character as spiritual adviser
North Carolina	8–53.2	according to the usual course of practice or discipline

Continued on next page

State	Code Citation	Qualifications
North Dakota	Rules of Evidence 505	made privately and not intended for further disclosure
Ohio	2317.02(C)	confidentially communicated, for purposes of religious counseling
Oklahoma	Ch. 12, 2505	made privately; clergy may claim privilege on behalf of another
Oregon	40.260	cannot be examined about communications made in professional character
Pennsylvania	Ch. 42, 5943	in usual course of duties
Puerto Rico	Rules of Evidence 28	made in confidence, in the course of discipline
Rhode Island	9-17-23	in professional character in course of discipline
South Carolina	19-11-90	in professional capacity, necessary and proper to enable clergy to discharge their office
South Dakota	19-13-16	made privately, not intended for further disclosure
Tennessee	24-1-206	clergy must be over 18; communicated in confidential manner
Texas	Rules of Evidence 505	in professional character as spiritual adviser
Utah	78-24-8	clergy cannot, without consent of person making confession, be examined as to any confession made in professional character
Vermont	Rules of Evidence 505	if made privately and not for further disclosure
Virginia	8.01-400 & 19.2-271.3	must be 18; usual course of practice or discipline
Virgin Islands	Tit. 5, Ch. 67, 857	made secretly, confidentially in course of discipline

State	Code Citation	Qualifications
Washington	5.60.06(3)	in professional character, in course of discipline
West Virginia	48-2-10a	both clergy and party made confidential statements in capacity as spiritual adviser
Wisconsin	905.06	clergy may claim privilege on behalf of another; professional character as spiritual adviser
Wyoming	1-12-101(a)(ii)	"confession" made to clergy in professional character

Table 5.1 is reprinted by permission of Human Sciences Press from a 1990 article in *Pastoral Psychology* by R. K. Bullis. Used by permission.

Table 5.2
Who Controls the Privilege?

State	Penitent Controls	Clergy Controls	Both Control
Alabama			X
Alaska	X		
Arizona	X		
Arkansas	by guardian or conservator or clergy		
California			X
Colorado			X
Connecticut	X		
Delaware	by guardian or conservator or clergy		
District of Columbia	X		
Florida	by guardian, conservator, personal representative, or clergy		
Georgia		clergy incompetent to testify	
Hawaii	by guardian, conservator, personal representative, or clergy		
Idaho	lawyer, guardian, conservator, personal representative (if deceased), or clergy		
Illinois		X	

State	Penitent Controls	Clergy Controls	Both Control
Indiana		clergy incompetent to testify	
Iowa	X		
Kansas	clergy on behalf of penitent		
Kentucky	X		
Louisiana	X		
Maine	by guardian, conservator, personal representative (if deceased), or clergy		
Maryland		X may not be compelled	
Massachusetts	X		
Michigan		clergy incompetent to testify	
Minnesota	X		
Mississippi	X		
Missouri		clergy incompetent to testify	
Montana	X		
Nebraska	by guardian, conservator, personal representative (if deceased), or clergy		
Nevada	X		
New Hampshire		X	
New Jersey			X

Continued on next page

State	Penitent Controls	Clergy Controls	Both Control
New Mexico	by guardian, conservator, personal representative (if deceased), or clergy		
New York	X		
North Carolina		clergy incompetent to testify	
North Dakota	by guardian, conservator, personal representative (if deceased), or clergy		
Ohio	X		
Oklahoma	by guardian, conservator, personal representative (if deceased), or clergy		
Oregon	X		
Pennsylvania	X		
Puerto Rico			X
Rhode Island	X		
South Carolina			X
South Dakota	X		
Tennessee			X
Texas	X		
Utah	X		
Vermont	by guardian, conservator, personal representative (if deceased), or clergy		
Virginia		cannot be required to give testimony	

State	Penitent Controls	Clergy Controls	Both Control
Virgin Islands	X		
Washington	X		
West Virginia	X		
Wisconsin	by guardian, conservator, personal representative (if deceased), or clergy		
Wyoming		clergy incompetent to testify	

6

LAWS LIMITING
THE CLERGY PRIVILEGE

*[The clergy privilege is] rooted in the imperative need for confidence
and trust. The priest-penitent privilege recognizes the human need to
disclose to a spiritual counselor, in total and absolute confidence, what
are believed to be flawed acts or thoughts and to receive priestly conso-
lation and guidance in return.*

—Chief Justice Burger

Introduction

Two kinds of laws serve to limit, influence, or inform clergy privileged
communications. First, child abuse reporting laws are in effect in all fifty
states, and these laws have exceptions for "spiritual healing." Second, as
discussed in prior chapters, religious counselors probably have a duty to
protect their counselees and to protect third parties who are in danger
from the counselee.

Child Abuse Reporting Laws

Child abuse reporting laws (CARL) have emerged as the prime statutes
limiting clergy privileged communications. (Bullis, 1990). CARL require
a broad spectrum of professionals to report suspected child abuse; they
define which professionals are "mandatory reporters." Civil and criminal penalties for mandatory reporters who do not comply are set forth.
In addition, immunities from suit are allowed for those who report suspected child abuse in good faith even if the report is erroneous.

CARL respond to society's compelling need to protect this vulnerable segment of the population. The New Jersey statute (§ 9:6-8.8, 1987)
states:

> The purpose of this act is to provide for the protection of children
> under 18 years of age who have had serious injury inflicted upon them
> by other than accidental means. It is the intent of this legislation to as-
> sure that the lives of innocent children are immediately safeguarded
> from further injury and possible death and that the legal rights of such
> children are fully protected.

New Jersey (§ 9:6-8.10, 1989) takes a very broad view of who must report:

> *Any person* having reasonable cause to believe that a child has been sub-
> jected to child abuse or acts of child abuse shall report the same imme-
> diately to the Division of Youth and Family Services by telephone or
> otherwise. (Emphasis added.)

Most CARL state that the report must be made promptly and specify to
whom the report must be made. The definition of child abuse, used in
New Jersey, is also typical of other states. New Jersey's broad definition
of child abuse includes acts that are physically or emotionally damaging
to the child, create a risk of harm, constitute sexual abuse, or fail to provide adequate food, clothing, shelter, education, medical care, or supervision for the child. (§ 9:6-8.9, 1987).

Religious counselors and others working for religious organizations
need to recognize that clergy communication is not always privileged,
particularly when suspected child abuse is present. Religious counselors
may want to tell penitents if there are limitations on the privacy of their
communication. Some believe that a penitent should be well apprised of
any limitations on the clergy person before the penitent confesses.

A growing minority of states also requires professionals to report
suspected incidents of elder abuse or abuse against the disabled. In reporting such abuse, the clergy privilege is either expressly or impliedly
negated. Alaska criminalizes both abuse against older citizens (aged
sixty-five or older) and physical or sexual assault of those who are
physically disabled. Clergy are mandatory reporters. (§ 47.24.010, 1990);
(§ 47.24.110, 1990).

Determining Legal Obligations to Report

This section addresses two issues crucial for clergy to understand and
apply CARL. The first issue involves whether clergy are defined as
mandatory reporters. Mandatory reporters are those classes of professionals who are required to report incidents of abuse. The second issue
delineates the exceptions to mandatory reporting.

Clergy as Mandatory and Permissive Reporters

Some states (such as New Jersey) require all of their citizens to report
suspected child abuse. Other states are less inclusive in defining mandatory reporters. For example, the South Carolina (§ 43-30-40, 1976) reporting law states:

> [a]ny physician, nurse, dentist, optometrist, medical examiner, coro-
> ner, or any other medical, mental health or allied health professional,
> *Christian Science practitioner, religious healer,* school teacher, counselor,

psychologist, mental health or mental retardation specialist, social or public assistance worker, or law enforcement officer. (Emphasis added.)

The specificity of this statute strongly suggests that clergy are not mandatory reporters, for they are not named. Christian Science practitioners are a class of trained persons accredited by that church. "Religious healers" is a less-defined term but seems to connote persons who have acquired special certification, training, or designation as healing intervenors.

Clergy working as teachers, public assistance workers, social workers, mental health practitioners, or as counselors may well be considered mandatory reporters. In the case of *State v. Motherwell*, mentioned in Chapter 1, two ministers, who were not yet ordained, were found to be in violation of the reporting statutes of Washington. The court found that their counseling fit the statutory definition of social workers who were designated as mandatory reporters. Both men were convicted.

Alabama's CARL (§ 26-14-3, 1986) state:

All hospitals, clinics, sanitariums, doctors, physicians . . . social workers, day care workers or employees, mental health professionals, or any other person called upon to render aid or medical assistance to any child, when such child is known or suspected to be a victim of child abuse or neglect, shall be required to report.

Clergy or other religious professionals are mandatory reporters if they are called upon to render aid to any child. Furthermore, Alabama (§ 26-14-10, 1986) requires testimony if the reporting leads to a trial:

The doctrine of privileged communication, with the exception of the attorney-client privilege, shall not be a ground for excluding any evidence regarding a child's injuries or the cause thereof in any judicial proceeding resulting from a report.

All states criminalize the failure to report child abuse for *mandatory* reporters. Failure to report generally results in a misdemeanor punishable with fines, imprisonment and/or probation, and possibly, as in the *Motherwell* case, a period of mandatory education. Judges may also impose a period of community service.

In addition to being prosecuted by the state under criminal law, the victim or the victim's guardian may sue for compensation under civil law. For instance, in one case the court found that a physician was negligent in failing to diagnose and report child abuse. (*Landeros v. Flood*, 1976). The doctor possessed sufficient knowledge of child abuse to recognize it, stated the court, and a reasonable person in similar circumstances would have recognized the abuse due to the extent of the injuries. Moreover, it was reasonable to assume that the abuse would continue if not reported. Clergy, particularly those involved in counseling or in mental health–related activities, are expected to have the opportunity and training to recognize child abuse. A permissive reporter is one who is allowed at his/her option to report child abuse. Clergy have legal status as permissive reporters in every state.

States that Require Both Mandatory Reporting and a Duty of Confidentiality to the Penitent

Florida, like New Jersey, requires everyone to report child abuse. Clergy are mandatory reporters, as are all other citizens. Florida law (§ 827.07[4], 1991) reads:

> *Any* person, including but not limited to, any physician, nurse, teacher, social worker, or employee of a public or private facility serving children, who has reason to believe that a child has been subject to abuse shall report or cause reports to be made to the department. (Emphasis added.)

Florida also requires clergy confidentiality to the penitent (§ 90.505, 1988):

> A communication between a clergyman and a person is "confidential" if made privately for the purpose of seeking spiritual counsel and advice from the clergyman in the usual course of his practice or discipline and not intended for further disclosure except to other persons present in furtherance of the communication.
>
> (2) A person has a privilege to refuse to disclose, and to prevent another from disclosing, a confidential communication by the person to a clergyman in his capacity as spiritual advisor.
>
> (3) The privilege may be claimed by:
>
> (a) The person.
> (b) The guardian or conservator of a person.
> (c) The personal representative of a deceased person.
> (d) The clergyman, on behalf of the person. The clergyman's authority to do so is presumed in the absence of evidence to the contrary.

Thus, at one time, in Florida, a religious counselor had a duty to report child abuse and a duty to keep a counselee's confidences.

In 1984, John Mellish, a pastor in Fort Lauderdale, refused to testify in Florida state court against a parishioner accused of child abuse. Mellish refused to testify to any matter related to his communications with his penitent. After a hearing on the confidentiality issue, the court ordered Mellish to divulge the information on the alleged abuse. The court found Mellish "in contempt"—a criminal charge punishable with fines and jail time. Mellish was sentenced to sixty days in jail; however, he served only twenty-four hours. (Cole, 1987). One year later, while Mellish was appealing his contempt conviction, the Florida legislature amended its law specifically to exempt clergy from reporting child abuse (§ 415.512, 1986) and the court dismissed Mellish's appeal.

Although Florida has settled the conflict and the case of Pastor Mellish, the issues that they raise are not moot. Florida's law exempting clergy from testifying in child abuse cases is an exception. Not every state requiring clergy to report child abuse has such a clear-cut law regarding clergy obligations. Many of the state statutes set forth a duty to report child abuse as well as a duty not to testify regarding privileged communications. Although closely related, *reporting* child abuse is different from *testifying* to alleged abuse in a court action, but this distinction has never been fully elaborated upon in the courts or in the statutes.

Some states have issued legal opinions, not arising from either court cases or statutory laws—such as the Texas Attorney General's opinion that clergy are not exempt from testifying in child abuse cases. (Silas, 1986). This lack of clarity gives rise to much confusion. One author (Cole, 1987, 3), after a careful examination of both CARL and clergy privileged communication statutes, asserted:

> [M]any states' child abuse reporting statutes, more as a result of inadvertence than design, do sweep members of the clergy into the category of persons obliged to report and testify about abuse, at least as a prima facie matter.

The above author also asserted that the obligation to report does not necessarily yield to the obligation to keep confidences. Current reporting statutes may be unconstitutional, however, because they create an impermissibly heavy burden on the clergy's free exercise of religion. To date, no clergy reporting statute has been challenged constitutionally.

Another author (Ivers, 1987) offered guidance to resolve potential conflicts between clergy privileged communication statutes and CARL. He suggested giving deference to the statute with the most compelling public policy, the more recently enacted, or the most specific statute. Where reporting laws require clergy to report and where clergy privileged communication is clearly abrogated by law, Ivers suggested that statutes may possibly be rewritten to require reporting only those abuse cases actually observed by the clergy.

State legislatures and judges will have to sift through competing societal interests. In the absence of clear, unconflicting statutory language, with or without an abrogation statute, the clergy person needs competent legal counsel. Where a review of statutes reveals uncertainty, preemptive legal advice is well worth the trouble.

Mistakes in Reporting: Can the Accused Retaliate?

The clergy person is immune from liability if she or he reports, in good faith, suspected child abuse that turns out to be false. The North Dakota statute (§ 50-25.1-09, 1989) illustrates:

> *Any person,* other than the alleged violator, participating in good faith in the making of a report . . . is immune from any liability, civil or criminal, that otherwise might result. For the purpose of any proceeding, civil or criminal, the good faith of any person required to report cases of child abuse or neglect shall be presumed. (Emphasis added.)

In New Jersey, Dr. Baron received a call from a hospital to treat a three-year-old with a leg fracture. After discussions with the parents, Dr. Baron made a child abuse report to the proper state agency. The division's investigation concluded that no abuse had taken place. The parents sued Dr. Baron for defamation, claiming that their reputation had been damaged. Two crucial facts helped the court rule that Dr. Baron was not liable. (*Rubinstein v. Baron,* 1987). First, New Jersey law absolutely immunizes those who in good faith report child abuse. This law presumes that reports are made in good faith. The burden of proving maliciousness by Dr. Baron was on the parents. In addition, both expert testimony and medical book evidence stated that these types of injuries were often consistent with injuries sustained in the course of child abuse.

Clergy who make reports should document observations of actual injuries, statements, dates, and places. Such information would both defend against a defamation claim and help investigators gather facts of abuse. Reports of abuse based exclusively upon second-hand information, hearsay, or unverifiable data may be less credible than eye-witness accounts, but they cause the reporter no legal problem when made in good faith.

The Spiritual Healing "Exception" to Child Abuse Laws

A clear majority of states statutorily exempt parents who use spiritual healing to cure childhood ills from child abuse prosecution. Parents, however, may be prosecuted nonetheless, as some state courts are narrowing their interpretation of these exemptions.

Table 6.1, located at the end of this chapter, lists the forty-six states that carry such laws, their code citations, and the relevant language of the statutes. (Bullis, 1991).

The state of Illinois (Ch. 23, § 2054, 1988) provides an example:

> A child whose parent, guardian or custodian in good faith selects and depends upon spiritual means through prayer alone for the treatment or cure of disease or remedial care may be considered negligent or abused, but not for the sole reason that his parent, guardian or custodian accepts and practices such beliefs.

Those who are responsible for a child can be held criminally responsible for a child's death in the event that they rely on spiritual means to cure the child; however, those responsible for the child may not be convicted *solely* because they relied on spiritual means. Other abusive factors must be present. The Illinois legislature tried to reconcile two important public policy goals in this law: the prevention of child abuse and the free exercise of religion. Thus, religious counselors may not have a duty to report suspected child abuse that is related solely to spiritual healing practices. If a religious counselor wanted to report such activity as abuse, thereby letting the authorities decide if abuse were present, then the good faith exception would probably support such action.

Conclusion: Practice Principles

There are two types of laws that limit the religious counselor's privilege to remain silent and keep confidences. First, religious counselors are bound by the laws discussed here regarding the duty to report statutorily defined cases of suspected abuse. The exception to this limitation is the exemption for parents following the advice or practices of spiritual healers. Second, religious counselors are bound by laws requiring them to protect others who may be endangered by their counselees and may even have a duty to protect self-destructive counselees. Refer to Chapters 2 and 3 for a discussion of the states that have been imposing a duty to warn and to protect on some counselors.

A series of questions can help determine the legal responsibilities of religious counselors under the CARL. Each question should be answered completely by someone with legal knowledge about the state where the religious counselor practices.

1. How does your state define clergy?

2. Are you a mandatory or permissive child abuse reporter under the laws of your state?

3. Are there other laws that require you to report suspected abuse, such as elder abuse or abuse of the mentally ill?

4. Who must you report to?

5. How quickly must you report?

6. Does the statute specify what type of evidence the report is to be based upon?

7. Do the reporting laws conflict with your state's clergy privileged communication law? If so, how would you resolve the conflict if you were required to report suspected abuse and were required to maintain confidences?

8. Suppose you are a permissive reporter and are required to maintain confidences. Is there a way to make a report?

References

Bullis, R. K. (1991). The Spiritual Healing "Defense" in Criminal Prosecutions for Crimes Against Children. *Child Welfare, 70*(5), 541–555. Table 6.1 is used by permission of the Child Welfare League of America.

———. (1990). Swallowing the Scroll: Legal Implications of the Recent Supreme Court Peyote Cases. *Journal of Psychoactive Drugs, 22*(3), 325–332.

Cole, W. A. (1987). Religious Confidentiality and the Reporting of Child Abuse: A Statutory and Constitutional Analysis. *Columbia Journal of Law and Social Problems, 21*(1), 1–51.

Ivers, W. N. (1987). When Must a Priest Report Under a Child Abuse Reporting Statute?—Resolution to the Priests' Conflicting Duties. *Valparaiso University Law Review, 21*, 431–465.

Landeros v. Flood, 17 Cal. App. 3d 399, 551 P.2d 389, 131 Cal. Rptr. 69 (1976).

Rubinstein v. Baron, 219 N.J. Super. 129, 529 A.2d 1061 (1987).

Silas, F. A. (1986). Embattled Clergy. *American Bar Association Journal, 72*, 36.

Table 6.1
Statutory Spiritual Healing "Exceptions" by State

State	Citation	Exceptions
Alabama (Michie 1986)	26-14-1	court can order medical treatment
Alaska (1989)	11.51.120	recognized church or denomination
Arizona (West 1989)	8-531.01	"duly accredited practitioner"
Arkansas (Michie 1987)	5-27-221	recognized church or denomination
California (1988)	Penal Tit. 9, 270	recognized church or denomination
Colorado (Bradford 1986 & Supp. 1989)	19-1-114	"duly accredited practitioner"
Connecticut (West Supp. 1989)	17-38d	only "accredited Christian Science practitioner"
Delaware (Michie 1985)	31, Section 401	recognized church or denomination
Florida (West 1990)	415.503	"legitimately practicing religious beliefs" *and* 1. does not negate "reporting" requirement 2. state may investigate 3. state may order treatment by physician or accredited practitioner
Georgia	None located	
Hawaii	350-2	"duly accredited practitioner"
Idaho (Michie 1987)	18-401	"treatment by prayer or spiritual means"
Illinois (Smith-Hurd 1988)	23, Section 2054	"spiritual means through prayer alone"

State	Citation	Exceptions
Indiana	35-46-1-4	"legitimate practice" of religion
Iowa (West Supp. 1989)	726.6(d)	interested party may petition the court for medical treatment
Kansas (1981)	21-3608(c)	recognized church or denomination
Kentucky (Michie Supp. 1988)	600.020(1)	court can order medical services
Louisiana (West Supp. 1990)	14:403	"well-recognized method" with a "reasonable proven record of success"
Maine (West Supp. 1989)	Tit. 22, 4010	"accredited practitioner of a recognized religious organization"
Maryland (Michie Supp. 1989)	Family Law 5-701(b)(2) and (n)(2)	"nonmedical remedial care"
Massachusetts (Lawyer's Co-op Supp. 1989)	Ch. 273, 1 (4)	recognized church or denomination
Michigan (West Supp. 1989)	722.634, Sect. 14	court may order "medical services or nonmedical remedial services"
Minnesota (West 1990)	626.556(c)	duty to report if child is in "imminent and serious" danger
Mississippi (Lawyer's Co-op Supp. 1989)	43-21-105(m)	judge may take jurisdiction in "best interest of child"
Missouri (West 1983)	210.115(3)	court may order "medical services" when child's health so requires
Montana (1989)	41-3-102(4)	"nonmedical remedial health care"
Nebraska	None located	

Continued on next page

State	Citation	Exceptions
Nevada (Michie 1986)	200.5085	"nonmedical remedial treatment"
New Hampshire (Equity 1989)	1169-C:3(c)	recognized church or denomination
New Jersey (West 1976)	9:6-1.1	rules for contagious diseases cannot be violated
New Mexico (Michie 1989)	32-1-3(L)(5) and (M)(4)	recognized church or denomination
New York (McKinney's 1989)	Penal Law 260.15	practitioner must be member or adherent of an organized church that prescribes prayer as the "principal" treatment for illness
North Carolina (Michie 1989)	Judicial 7A-517(21)	"other remedial care"
North Dakota (Michie 1989)	50-25.1(2)	court may order medical services
Ohio (Page's Supp. 1989)	2919.22(A)	recognized religious body
Oklahoma (West 1990)	Ch. 29, 852(A)	court may assume custody to protect child's health or welfare
Oregon (Butterworth 1987)	419.500(1)	court may maintain jurisdiction
Pennsylvania (Purdon Supp. 1989)	Tit. 11, 2203	recognized church or denomination
Rhode Island (Michie 1984)	40-11-15	court can order medical services
South Carolina (Lawyer's Co-op 1985)	20-7-490(C)(3)	"nonmedical remedial health care"
South Dakota (Allen Smith 1984)	26-10-1.1	recognized church through accredited practitioner
Tennessee	None located	

State	Citation	Exceptions
Texas	None located	
Utah (Michie 1987)	78-3a-19.5	"legitimately practicing beliefs"
(Michie 1989)	26-23-10	sanitary laws must be satisfied
Vermont (Equity Supp. 1989)	Tit. 33, 682(C)	legitimately practicing religious beliefs
Virginia (Michie Supp. 1989)	16.1-228(2)	recognized church or denomination
Washington (West 1989)	26.44.020	Christian Science practitioner
West Virginia (West 1989)	49-1-3(2)(A)	recognized religious denomination of which parent or guardian is adherent or member
Wisconsin (West 1987)	48.981(4)	"due regard to culture" and court may order medical services if child's health so requires
Wyoming (Michie 1986)	14-3-202(a)(vii)	"duly accredited practitioner"

7

GENERAL TRENDS AND PATTERNS
OF RELIGIOUS COUNSELING LIABILITY

If nowhere else, in the relation between Church and State, "good fences make good neighbors."
                                                              —*Felix Frankfurter*

Overview

As stated previously, there are three arenas where religious counselors are particularly susceptible to suit. First, religious counselors are susceptible when, for various reasons, they discuss openly matters they have learned from private counseling sessions with the counselee, or when they fail to report such matters when they are obligated to do so by state law. The second category of behavior for which religious counselors are being sued involves the content or quality of the advice given during counseling sessions. (Taylor, 1990). This area involves the duty to protect the counselee, the duty to warn third parties of danger from the counselee, and the duty to give sound counseling advice. Finally, distinguishable from the counselor's advice, the counselor's conduct (i.e., sexual contact with the counselee) is increasingly giving rise to suits against the religious counselor. (Taylor, 1990).

Issues Related to Confidentiality

The counselee can sue the religious counselor in an effort to prevent the religious counselor from informally disseminating the counselee's confidential information, to prevent the testifying or suppress testimony by the religious counselor, or to receive damages to compensate for the harm resulting from disclosure. The religious counselor's duty of confidentiality may also extend to a third party. If, for example, a religious counselor revealed that a counselee's ex-husband was threatening to kill someone, it might be possible for the ex-husband to bring suit against the religious counselor. Finally, a counselee might be able to convince a court that she should receive punitive damages, which are assessed for the sole purpose of chastisement.

Alternatively, the religious counselor may be subject to contempt proceedings for refusing to breach a confidence when under legal order to do so. When the religious counselor is under a legal duty to report child abuse and does not do so, the religious counselor is not only subject to legal action from the state but is also subject to suit by the child, especially if the abuse continues.

The legal issues surrounding clergy confidentiality are complicated by three duties the religious counselor faces: (1) the duty to maintain the confidences of the counselee; (2) the duty to obey the law and court orders; and (3) the duty to the victim or potential victim of any threatened or continued harm. In order to make sense of the various court decisions, it is helpful to categorize the cases in the following manner.

The Confidence Sought to Be Maintained Involves Admission of a Criminal Act Already Committed

When a person seeks religious counseling after committing a criminal act, the police may ask the clergy to testify before a grand jury investigation. Where the crime is completed, with no likelihood of further harm, maintaining the confidence may be preferred. In Pittsburgh, a fire broke out in a house that had recently been purchased by a black family located in an all-white neighborhood. Arson was suspected. (*In re Grand Jury*, 1990). Shortly after the fire, a family of four living next to the burned home sought counseling with a Lutheran minister. The family included two married adults, a son of the married woman, and his fiancée.

The federal circuit court determined that the pastor did not have to divulge the nature of the meetings he had had with the four, although the court questioned whether each individual present was necessary to the meeting. Had one member, the fiancée for instance, not been essential to the counseling session, her presence would waive the entire family's claim to privilege. The court remanded (i.e., sent) the case back to the lower court for fact finding on the issue of each party's essential nature to the counseling session.

Similarly, in another case, a minister learned that her nephew had been arrested for rape. (*State v. Jackson*, 1985). She visited him "both as a close relative and as a minister" and received his confession at the jail. The court determined that because it was impossible to tell to what extent the confession was elicited because the aunt was a minister, the entire communication was privileged.

Although there is greater sympathy for allowing the minister to maintain the privilege when the suspected crime is completed and the harm is not continuing, the weight of the crime will also figure into the equation. Additionally, the need for the minister's testimony will be scrutinized. Sufficient evidence from other sources will render the minister's testimony superfluous.

If the need for the testimony is great or if there is a serious public outcry over the crime, the court will normally look for ways to construe the privilege very narrowly. As mentioned earlier, if a religious counselor refuses to testify, he/she may be subject to civil or criminal sanctions including fines and/or jail time imposed by the court. If the religious counselor continues to refuse to honor the court order, he/she will stay in jail until the time is served or until the court relents.

Maintaining the Confidence May Well Lead to Continuing Harm or Imminent Future Harm

In some cases, the religious counselor will assert the right not to disclose confidential information even when continuing harm may be the result. More recently, the courts are reluctant to allow this. It may be that the religious counselor is the only one who knows of a serious ongoing problem and therefore is the only hope the victim has for "rescue."

A priest doing counseling with prisoners on Rikers Island was summoned to testify before a grand jury that was investigating allegations of corruption in the prison parole system. (*Keenan v. Gigante*, 1979). The priest refused to testify, stating that his job of counseling involved interceding with government officials and would be confidential. The court disagreed, finding that the information being elicited focused solely on his own conversation. The judge committed him to prison for ten days.

Repeatedly, church officials allege that because knowledge comes to them through confession, they are immune from suit for failure to reveal a person's harmful proclivities. In one case, a religious counselor knew that a bus driver had a history of sexually assaulting young girls but agreed to counsel him in exchange for his driving the church bus for the youth group. (*J. v. Victory Tabernacle Baptist Church*, 1988). The bus driver began molesting one of the children on the bus, and the minister should have been alert to this potential problem. When the clergy person, because of information gleaned from the counseling relationship, is the critical link in preventing harm to innocent third parties, the privileged communication defense is less favored.

Intentional Disclosure to the Public
of the Counselee's Private Confessions

When a religious counselor for his/her own personal reasons chooses to violate a counselee's confidentiality and intentionally makes known private information to the general public, the courts have refused to grant religious immunity to the religious counselor. In one case, a bishop and his former lover sued the Evangelical Orthodox Church for disclosing their sexual liaison to his congregation. (*Snyder v. Evangelical Orthodox Church*, 1989). This information, gained through the bishop's confession after he was promised confidentiality, was announced from the pulpit. Later, those members who had not attended worship were visited and individually informed of the news.

The church and its leaders did not deny the disclosure, stating only that the plaintiffs' complaint intimately involved the doctrines, teachings, and practices of the church and was off-limits to the court. Interestingly, the laws providing for clergy confidentiality were formulated in an effort to avoid excessive entanglement with religion. The church, in this instance, argued that in an effort to avoid excessive entanglement, it should be allowed to breach such confidentialities. The court disagreed.

In a case mentioned in Chapter 5, *Hester v. Barnett*, the court found that there would be no religious immunity where the religious counselor induced a family to confide in him, with the promise of confidentiality. The religious counselor disclosed some of the family's problems and some untruths to the public. Although the court refused to recognize claims for clergy malpractice, negligent counseling, or breach of confidentiality, the court readily found viable claims for unreasonable intrusion upon the seclusion of another. Where the breach of confidentiality appears based on a desire to humiliate, punish, or be vindictive, the courts refuse to allow a religious immunity defense.

Issues Related to the Content and Quality
of the Religious Counselor's Advice

Advice that animates destructive or life-changing behavior is particularly at risk for allegations that the counseling was per se ineffective. These suits are often filed by the loved ones of a counselee who has committed suicide or has requested a divorce, or by the counselee who in retrospect believes that the religious counselor did not have the counselee's best interest at heart. These plaintiffs usually sue for extensive damages.

Nally, discussed in Chapter 2, exemplifies the case of a religious counselor who was sued for the content of the advice given. The pastors in *Nally* were accused of advising Nally that suicide was an acceptable alternative if one was failing to live up to Christian standards. Additionally, the pastors were accused of failing to give proper advice, that is, failing to refer Nally to a psychiatrist and failing to warn his family and doctors of his continuing desire to kill himself.

The pastoral advice in Nally was alleged to have been reckless and callous. In other cases, the advice is unabashedly self-dealing. In one case, a woman who was falling behind in her mortgage payments "turned to her pastor . . . in whom she had trust and confidence, for counsel and advice." (*Adams v. Moore*, 1989). After assuring her that he could help her, the pastor, with another pastor, advised her that if she would deed the home to them, they would pay her two thousand dollars and assume the mortgage. A few months later, they sold the home for thirty-two thousand dollars. The court found that the pastor had breached a fiduciary relationship to the counselee because she had reposed a special confidence in him. The pastor was bound to act in good faith and with due regard for her interests.

In addition to advice that is self-dealing, courts are suspicious of advice that essentially harms the counselee. Some courts have had to examine allegations that religious counselors have advised women to divorce or emotionally harm their spouses. In one Idaho case, $750,000 was initially awarded to a father and his children when he sued a church, its bishop, its priest, and some of the church members for essentially breaking up his marriage. (*O'Neil v. Schuckardt*, 1986). The defendants advised the wife that her marriage was not valid in the eyes of God because the husband's religion was wrong. The wife was told that she could not have sexual relations with her husband as this would be a sin, and if she found herself acting as a wife, it was her duty to leave her husband. The court determined that "[g]ood faith and reasonable conduct are the necessary touchstones to . . . any invited and religiously direct family counseling." Reckless recommendations of family separation, generally speaking, can be a basis for liability.

Two million dollars in punitive damages alone was awarded to a church member who received destructive counseling from his church. (*Wollersheim v. Church of Scientology*, 1992). Wollersheim was a manic depressive with an obvious susceptibility to mental disorder; indeed, at one point he was considering suicide. Nonetheless, he was counseled by his church that he should never speak of his problems with a doctor, psychiatrist, or priest of another faith. He was also told to cease contact with his family. In an attempt to punish him for leaving the church and to force him to stay with the church, information gleaned from his confidential religious sessions was publicly disclosed. The court found that the church was liable for infliction of emotional injury and would not recognize a religious immunity defense.

Courts are less and less amenable to a First Amendment, separation of church and state, defense when a religious counselor is involved in intentionally harming, defrauding, and overreaching the counselee.

Issues Related to the Religious Counselor's Sexual Contact with the Counselee

Any counselor who has sexual contact with a counselee exposes him/herself to great risk of suit. Courts have reviewed charges that the role of the religious counselor heightens the element of coercion. Normally, the counselee and/or the counselee's spouse will bring suit for failure to fulfill the fiduciary duty owed to the counselee. These suits involve compensatory and punitive damages. It should be mentioned that a criminal action, as distinguished from a civil action discussed here, will be brought by the state when the counselee is a minor. Ancillary civil suits may be brought by the parents of the minor. Thus, sexual contact with a minor, which is without question against the law, must be distinguished from sexual contact with an adult, which may or may not be considered illegal conduct.

Sexual Contact Is Becoming Synonymous with Misconduct

Nine states have determined that sexual contact with a counselee is a criminal act by the therapist. Additionally, four states have passed laws making therapist-patient sexual contact a civil offense. Some states that do not have criminal and civil statutes specifically prohibiting this conduct have found the religious counselor liable based on torts of outrageous conduct or breach of fiduciary duty to the counselee.

Furthermore, other statutes criminalizing sexual behavior must be considered; for example, the laws against adultery and fornication are still viable in some states. It is also important to focus on ethical obligations. The American Psychiatric Association's Ethics Committee states that sexual contact between the counselor and counselee always involves problems of transference. As such, the time of commencement of a sexual relationship is irrelevant.

More and more of these counselees are taking their claims to court and winning. In Oregon, a church parishioner sued her pastor, alleging breach of confidential relationship and intentional infliction of severe emotional distress. She stated that the pastor mentally manipulated her to become dependent on him and seduced her for his own purposes through the counseling relationship. (*Erickson v. Christenson*, 1989).

The plaintiff was thirteen when the sexual contact began. Their intimate relationship lasted sixteen years. The pastor argued that the claim could not stand because (1) it was in essence a claim for seduction, which had been abolished; (2) it was in essence a claim for clergy malpractice, which would entail interference with clerical counseling and was not a recognized claim in any state; and (3) their sexual relationship would not give rise to liability were it not for the fact that he was a minister; therefore, he was being penalized for exercising his religion. The court found the minister's defenses to be without merit and allowed the plaintiff's complaint to go forward.

In Colorado, a divorced couple brought an action against a priest because the priest, after asserting that they could trust him as a marital counselor, engaged in sexual conduct with the wife during the term of the marriage counseling. (*Destefano v. Grabrian,* 1988). The priest had stated that he was a capable, trained professional counselor who could be relied upon to act in the best interest of the counselees. The court, a special panel involving all of the state's supreme court judges, determined that the priest had a fiduciary duty to both of the counselees. As such, the clergyman was under a fiduciary obligation not to do anything that might harm the marital relationship. The court refused to recognize clergy malpractice as a claim, but also refused to allow the First Amendment to immunize the priest's actions. The claim of sexual misconduct, stated the court, could be considered the tort of outrageous conduct causing severe emotional distress even though the state no longer recognized any tort for alienation of affections.

Sexual Misconduct by a Religious Counselor Is Sometimes Protected as Religious Activity Under the Constitution

Numerous cases alleging clergy sexual misconduct are dismissed for being in essence heart balm claims (e.g., seduction), which have been abolished in many states. From time to time, however, when the court dismisses a sexual misconduct complaint, First Amendment protections appear to buttress the court's reasoning.

In a case somewhat similar to *Erickson,* mentioned above, Schmidt alleged that her pastor had initiated sexual contact with her during a counseling relationship. The counseling began when she was twelve, and she became emotionally dependent on the minister. The relationship terminated when Schmidt was forty, two years before she filed suit. (*Schmidt v. Bishop,* 1991). The court listed religious immunity as one of the reasons that it would dismiss the complaint. The court admitted that it required no excessive entanglement with religion to decide that reasonably prudent clergy of any sect do not molest children. Nonetheless, the court insisted that it was bound by the First Amendment to grant immunity to the pastor.

In *Handley v. Richards* (1987), the husband of a couple receiving marriage counseling committed suicide after he discovered that his wife was having an affair with the religious counselor. His next of kin, claiming outrageous conduct and clergy malpractice, alleged that the suicide was caused by the "deceitful manner of the counseling" conducted by the religious counselor. Although two judges dismissed the complaint without an opinion, a third judge wrote separately to make clear that, in his opinion, which was a minority, there would be no First Amendment protections for such conduct. The judge summarily stated that he would dismiss the case because the minister's misconduct did not rise to a level of "outrageous conduct" for purposes of bringing a legal action.

Conclusion

Religious counselors are being sued because of issues related to confidentiality, content of advice, and sexual misconduct. Pursuant to First Amendment protections, the courts have unanimously refused to examine whether a minister's conduct conforms to the "standard" expected of a minister. It is unlikely that a court will ever animate this standard. Instead, the courts are basing decisions of religious counselor liability on allegations simultaneously involving intentional torts such as breach of fiduciary duty, outrageous conduct, or invasion of privacy. Further complicating this area of the law is the fact that when the court signals in an interim ruling that it is legally disposed toward the plaintiff who is suing a religious counselor, the cases settle with extreme swiftness. Normally, the court's involvement and further public knowledge of the case cease. Nonetheless, whether examining intentional breach of confidence, ineffective advice, or sexual contact, the courts generally appear to be using a standard that measures the malice of the religious counselor and the harm rendered to the counselee.

References

Adams v. Moore, 96 N.C. App. 359, 385 S.E.2d 799 (1989), *rev. denied*, 326 N.C. 46, 389 S.E.2d 83 (1990).

Destefano v. Grabrian, 763 P.2d 275 (Colo. 1988).

Erickson v. Christenson, 99 Or. App. 104, 781 P.2d 383 (1989), *appeal dismissed*, 311 Or. 266, 817 P.2d 758 (1991).

Handley v. Richards, 518 So.2d 682 (Ala. 1987).

In re Grand Jury Investigation, 918 F.2d 374 (3d Cir. 1990).

J. v. Victory Tabernacle Baptist Church, 236 Va. 206, 372 S.E.2d 391 (1988).

Keenan v. Gigante, 47 N.Y.2d 160, 390 N.E.2d 1151, 417 N.Y.S.2d 226 (1979).

O'Neil v. Schuckardt, 112 Idaho 472, 733 P.2d 693 (1986).

Schmidt v. Bishop, 779 F. Supp. 321 (S.D.N.Y. 1991).

Snyder v. Evangelical Orthodox Church, 216 Cal. App. 3d 297, 264 Cal. Rptr. 640 (1989).

State v. Jackson, 77 N.C. App. 832, 336 S.E.2d 437 (1985).

Taylor, M. (1990). *Nally v. Grace Community Church:* The Future of Clergy Malpractice Under Content-Based Analysis. *Utah Law Review, 1990,* 661–683.

Wollersheim v. Church of Scientology, 4 Cal. App. 4th 1074, 6 Cal. Rptr. 2d 532 (1992).

8

A LEGAL AUDIT

FOR RELIGIOUS COUNSELORS

Do not, as some ungracious pastors do,
Show me the steep and thorny way to heaven,
Whiles, like a puff'd and reckless libertine,
Himself the primrose path of dalliance treads,
And recks not his own rede.

—*Shakespeare*, Hamlet

To Breach or Not to Breach?

Balancing The Interests

Who Will Be Damaged?

There are a number of questions that may help to clarify whether breaching a confidence is wise. Decide who will be damaged if the minister remains silent. Conversely, determine who will be damaged if the minister breaches the confidentiality.

In 1855, the Very Reverend Teeling was summoned to testify regarding a deathbed confession that he heard from a woman who had been fatally wounded. The man accused of killing her was her husband. The court summoned the priest to give any information that would assist it in determining the husband's guilt or innocence. The priest refused, stating that any statement made by the wife either exculpating or inculpating the accused would not be revealed.

The court decided that the priest could not be forced to testify, even though the confession it sought to uncover was of a woman no longer living, and another person's life hung in the balance. (Stokes, 1975). It is helpful in this area, to decide whose confidence will be breached. For example, some states require disclosure of child abuse when the counselee is the victim but not if the counselee is the abuser.

Put Child Abuse in a Special Category

Make a clear demarcation between disclosing child abuse and disclosing other matters. In cases where a minister reveals a counselee's confidences, normally there is a great deal of public outrage. The narrow exception to this is the reporting of child abuse, where obviously young, innocent victims are at stake. In *People v. Edwards,* mentioned in Chapter 5, the minister reported to church elders that the counselee had embezzled $30,000 from church funds. The public vilified the pastor even though the court found that the pastor had not violated any law.

Although the majority of states do not include clergy as mandatory reporters, virtually every state authorizes the *voluntary* disclosure of child abuse. Thus, in this one area, the minister is encouraged to breach the counselee's confidences. Review the state statute regarding the legal duty to report child abuse. Determine whether there is a time period within which the religious counselor has to report such knowledge or suspicions.

In situations where suspicion or knowledge of child abuse is obtained from the victim, the temptation to play detective is great. The religious counselor may know the family members well. In a recent case in New York, the religious counselor could not reconcile the daughter's allegations with his perception of the father. The religious counselor saw his role as ascertaining the truth, which he believed was synonymous with the exoneration of the father. He repeatedly asked the slightly retarded girl to admit she was lying.

The pastor has no authority to investigate or to discount a complaint of child abuse. Indeed, the religious counselor who interferes with a witness's statements is illegally tampering with evidence. Thus, even if the pastor does not believe the child, the incident must be reported. In the above case, the child recanted, and the minister felt like a hero. Instead, the religious counselor broke the law for failing to report the statements to the proper authorities. Rather than investigating it her/himself, the religious counselor must turn the case over to the authorities. The child should be provided with as much support as possible. The religious counselor's records should reflect that evidence or statements of abuse have surfaced in counseling and that certain authorities have been contacted, with the specific date, time, and persons contacted.

Reflect on What Is Right for the Specific Situation

The Religious Counselor Wants to Break a Confidence

The religious counselor must determine his/her goal. In some cases, the religious counselor may decide that he/she has a duty to the counselee or to a third party that outweighs the duty of confidentiality. If the religious counselor determines that breaching the confidence is the proper response, then the privilege statute should be consulted. Often the domain of the statute will be limited to in-court testimony and will be silent as to all other situations. The privilege may not even extend to testimony for a grand jury investigation. Police, family members, third parties, social agencies, and so forth, could be contacted without breaching the statute. Nonetheless, the religious counselor would be wise to expect to be sued. The counselee may, of course, bring a tort action based on breach of fiduciary duty, breach of confidentiality, breach of contract, or invasion of privacy. The success of such a suit would depend on the facts of the case.

A breach of confidentiality to the counselee is probably acceptable if the religious counselor (1) has the client's permission; (2) has been summoned by the state or federal government to testify; (3) is under an obligation or is authorized to report child abuse; or (4) has a clear indication that the client is a threat to him/herself or others. It is also likely that a court would permit the counselor to breach a duty of confidentiality if the client were suing the pastor over some matter related to the counseling session. A pastor would have a right to defend him/herself to the fullest extent.

The religious counselor must make clear to the counselee if their relationship is not religious in nature and therefore no expectation of confidentiality should ensue. In one case, a rabbi was called to testify in the trial of a man accused of murdering his young wife. (*People v. Drelich*, 1986). The rabbi had stressed many times to the accused, during their talks at the jail, that his role was not rabbinical in nature, and that he would not have involved himself in the matter otherwise. The court found the sessions between the rabbi and the accused to be secular in nature. The religious counselor should think through his/her role and discuss this bluntly with the counselee.

No court has found a pastor liable for breaching confidentiality to save another from harm, and it is unlikely that such a suit would be successful. Thus, if a person confides to the religious counselor that he/she will or wants to harm a specific person, the religious counselor probably can reveal this information to the police, the person subject to threat of harm, the parents if a minor is involved, and/or the counselee's spouse if this will assist in averting the danger. Even solid legal principles supporting the religious counselor's desire to disclose, however, will not necessarily prevent the counselee, whose confidences have been revealed, from filing suit.

The Religious Counselor Wants to Remain Silent

If the religious counselor determines that maintaining the counselee's confidence is the proper response, then he/she should read the privilege statute. Statutes will often distinguish between civil and criminal matters. The state has a greater interest in ascertaining the truth when a person's life and liberty are at stake. Thus, if it is a civil matter, the state may be less interested in compelling the minister to testify. As mentioned above, the statutes often address only the religious counselor's right to maintain confidentiality in court settings. If the statute is too narrow for the religious counselor's situation and the pastor wants to remain silent, the pastor could assert the right to confidentiality based on the First Amendment.

Aside from mandatory reporting cases, no court has found a pastor liable for failing to warn someone of imminent harm based on knowledge learned from the confidential counseling session. Many courts are reluctant to find fault with a minister who maintains secrecy, regardless of the consequences. In one such case, a minister was counseling his church's youth director, who admitted molesting four children who lived next door to him. (*Miller v. Everett*, 1991). The molestation occurred before, during, and after the counseling. The parents sued the minister, alleging that he had a duty to warn them and the authorities of future criminal activity that was clearly foreseeable. The court found that the minister had no duty to control the counselee for the benefit of a third party absent a special relationship to the third party.

Content and Quality of Counseling

Recognizing which counseling situations are most likely to expose the religious counselor to the risk of being sued is important. Suicidal counselees make the religious counselor vulnerable to suit by family members and loved ones if the counselee takes his/her life. Counselees who are noncompliant or violent may harm themselves or others and give rise to allegations that the religious counseling was per se ineffective.

Counseling courses regarding the suicidal or self-destructive client would be beneficial for the religious counselor as well as learning to recognize the signs for the suicidal and/or violent state of mind. Probably the best way for the religious counselor to begin would be to take a thorough personal history of the counselee.

Once the religious counselor recognizes that the person is suicidal, she/he should suggest additional assistance and consider personally taking the person to the doctor or arranging for a family member to do so. The religious counselor may want to maintain a list of counselors who are recognized by the state as specifically trained to treat the suicidal patient—that is, those who are authorized to administer medication and to initiate involuntary commitment proceedings.

Specificity in giving referrals and follow-up on the referrals are important. The religious counselor should notify a spouse, or parents, or family members who are involved with the counselee. If it is known that the person is under care of a doctor or a suicide-trained professional, the religious counselor should inform these professionals concerning the counselee's mental state.

It would be wise for the religious counselor to document his/her conversations with family members, referral attempts, and any warnings given to the police, family, or innocent third parties believed to be facing a threat of danger from the counselee. The religious counselor will want to maintain thorough records of the date and content of counseling visits. In the event of litigation, the records will help the religious counselor's memory and substantiate his/her position.

Sexual Contact with the Counselee

The authors strongly recommend against the dating of counselees. At the very minimum, however, the religious counselor should not date the counselee unless the following conditions are met: (1) there is no state law prohibiting sexual activity between the counselor and the counselee or former counselee; (2) there is no rule or policy adopted by the religious counselor's church, association, conference, or denomination that forbids dating counselees or parishioners; (3) there is no rule prohibiting such conduct promulgated by professional associations of which the religious counselor is a member; (4) therapy has been terminated six months prior to the first date; (5) issues of transference have been thoroughly examined and resolved; (6) there is a balance of power between the religious counselor and the counselee; *and* (7) the counselor has discussed this with a supervisor, peers, and church leadership if the counselee is a member of the congregation, and has documented these conversations.

Steps for Prevention

The most important preventative measure is, by far, for the religious counselor to take greater responsibility for the legal aspect of his/her ministry. There are many resources available today related to the legal aspects of one's counseling, and it is critical for the religious counselor to avail him/herself of them. Numerous professional bodies exist that will interpret the latest changes and additions to the relevant laws. These bodies will also help the religious counselor to network with other people who are knowledgeable in these areas.

The religious counselor must regularly attend continuing education in all legal aspects of counseling and professional ethics. Additional courses of special significance include privileged communications, mandatory reporting, duties and standards of care in religious counseling, issues related to sexual contact, and so forth. Continuing education workshops focusing on the legal ramifications of one's work are particularly useful when they highlight new trends or changes in the laws.

Other preventative measures include avoiding the performance or even the appearance of performing psychotherapy unless the state's requirements for such are satisfied. Assuming that the state requirements in question have not been met, the religious counselor must be careful to confine the counseling to religious guidance. The religious counselor may want to refer issues of sexual or family violence.

The religious counselor should obtain counseling supervision by a mentor and/or peer. Counseling more than four sessions with one person without supervision is not recommended. Nor is counseling more than eight hours a week without professional training. It follows that the religious counselor should join peer support groups, maintain memberships in professional counseling organizations, and receive and review the trade journals of these groups.

Record keeping is an important aspect of prevention. Records should be maintained for the counselor's lifetime. Recently, a thirty-four-year-old man sued a pastor who was in his late seventies, alleging criminal and civil misconduct that had its inception twenty-two years before. Some states have no statute of limitations for offenses involving molestation of a minor.

Before entering into a counseling relationship with a counselee, the religious counselor should discuss the idea of taking to a mediator or arbitrator any dispute that might arise from the counseling relationship. (Both of these can be located through the local or state bar association.) Any such agreement should be thoroughly discussed, should be in writing, and should be signed by both parties. Of course, an agreement like this would bind the religious counselor as well as the counselee (e.g., issues related to payment). Neither the religious counselor nor the counselee can contract away rights guaranteed by the criminal law system. Thus, if one physically attacked the other or vandalized property of the other, the prior contract agreeing not to go to court would not be enforceable.

Do Not Be Intimidated by the Threat of Litigation

Even when the religious counselor knows he/she is conducting counseling well within the confines of her legal and ethical duties, he should expect to be sued. The religious counselor should not panic: Being sued is not synonymous with guilt. The counselor will simply want to find a good lawyer, and stand his/her ground.

Use of a lawyer referral system to find a lawyer who is trained in the subject for which the religious counselor is being sued is recommended. The local or state bar association will be of assistance. Some religious counseling issues are so unique that finding a lawyer with a background in the particular problem will be extremely beneficial in procuring sound advice.

Even after the complaint is filed, the religious counselor may want to suggest that the disputants seek alternatives to the litigation process; for example, arbitration, mediation, and alternative dispute resolution.

The religious counselor may want to cultivate a relationship with an attorney with whom he/she is comfortable. It would be smart to seek this attorney's advice on a routine basis, before problems start or a situation grows out of control.

Malpractice Insurance

One of the most important aspects of the religious counselor's contract with his/her institution, if he/she is affiliated with one, is who will pay for the malpractice insurance and how much will be maintained. Malpractice insurance should be obtained at a level of at least one million dollars per occurrence; some suggest as high as fifty million. It should not be assumed that with a lighter load of counseling, the counselor could decrease this recommended minimum. The threat of suit is present with only one counselee.

Insurance generally will not cover deliberate acts. Coverage is intended only for those events that could not be prevented, that were unexpected and beyond one's control, or that occurred due to one's negligence. Normally, insurance will cover only civil suits. When a suit is instituted against the religious counselor and the counselor denies culpability, the insurance company may be under an obligation to provide an attorney who will defend the religious counselor in court. If the court case is dropped or is won by the religious counselor, the insurance company will pay for the legal fees. If the suit is lost by the religious counselor, whether the insurance company pays the damages and legal fees will be set forth in the policy. The insurance company probably would pay a certain amount of damages and fees in a negligence case but may not in a suit involving intentional acts.

The religious counselor should carefully review his/her malpractice insurance policy. He/She must ask the insurance agent questions regarding any part of the policy that is not understood. After reading the insurance policy and talking with the agent, the religious counselor should be able to answer the following questions:

1. Is counseling covered? What about full-time counseling?

2. Who is covered? Both the church and the pastor should have policies.

3. What types of perils is the religious counselor insured against?

4. What behavior or types of suits are excluded? Some policies will not cover suits alleging libel and slander, two important areas for the religious counselor. Others except from coverage licentious, immoral, or any acts intended to lead to a sexual act. Incidentally, one can procure through the American Counseling Association and the National Association of Social Workers insurance that covers some sexual misconduct.

5. Does the policy cover intentional acts?

6. Does it cover criminal or only civil lawsuits?

7. What period of time is covered by the policy; that is, what are the dates of inception and expiration? Distinguish between when the claim is filed and when the act occurred. For instance, once the coverage is terminated, will the insurance company defend the counselor if a suit arises many years later regarding counseling done when the policy was in effect?

8. Will the insurance company pay a lawyer to represent the religious counselor in a suit? Will the counselor be allowed to choose his/her own attorney? Will the company pay damages if the suit is lost? If so, how much?

9. Does the insurance company's duty to defend the counselor include a duty to appeal an adverse judgment? If the insurance company provides its own attorney to defend the religious counselor, that attorney is working for the insurance company and has the insurance company's interest as the first priority. Serious problems can flow from this: would a judgment against the counselor relieve the insurance company from paying on the claim?

10. Is the company under a duty to notify the counselor if the accuser makes an offer of settlement? Who has the final authority over settling the suit? Can it be settled without the religious counselor's consent? The insurance company may strategize that it can save money if it settles the claim instead of defending it. If this is the case, sometimes the religious counselor finds his/her reputation is sacrificed in the process.

11. Are defense costs included in the policy limits, and is the deductible set-off against defense costs?

12. Is the liability of the insurer limited by claim? Is there a lifetime or annual cap on the amount that the insurer will pay?

The premiums should be paid on time. Representations made when filling out the application that are material to the policy and are untrue or misleading can be grounds for the insurance company to void the policy later. Most jurisdictions and some policies explicitly state that there is a period after which the company can no longer raise contested facts in the application as a defense to coverage.

Ethical Codes

It would behoove the religious counselor to be familiar with the applicable codes of ethics. At least three professional organizations for clergy have promulgated codes of ethics: the American Association of Pastoral Counselors, the Christian Association for Psychological Studies, and the Association for Clinical Pastoral Education. Of course, these codes apply only to the members of each respective organization. Religious counselors may be aware of ethical codes arising from other affiliations, such as the American Association of Sex Educators, Counselors, and Therapists. There is a special obligation, as well, for religious counselors to adhere to the professional code of ethics promulgated by their denominational or licensing bodies.

Conclusion

In conclusion, the best legal advice for the religious counselor is the maxim: An ounce of prevention is worth a pound of cure. This volume familiarizes the reader with the potential trouble areas that need to be handled with extra care and awareness. It highlights and examines the three areas of conduct where religious counselors are most likely to be sued: (1) the religious counselor breaches a confidence or fails to reveal a confidence when under a legal duty to do so; (2) the content and quality of advice given by the religious counselor is questionable, involving the religious counselor's duty to protect the counselee and the duty to warn third parties of danger from the counselee; and (3) the religious counselor allegedly engages in sexual contact with the counselee. With this heightened awareness, the religious counselor can conduct his/her counseling activities with greater confidence and increased ability to recognize and avoid situations or conduct that may give rise to personal liability.

Following the suggestions for prevention and carrying sufficient malpractice insurance are two of the wisest measures a religious counselor can undertake. If the religious counselor is sued or is threatened with suit, there is no reason to panic. The counselor will want to contact his/her attorney immediately and also his/her insurance company. This volume will provide the religious counselor with a good basis for understanding the case and for maintaining a sense of control or order amidst the unfolding events.

References

Miller v. Everett, 576 So.2d 1162 (La. 1991).

People v. Drelich, 123 A.D.2d 441, 506 N.Y.S.2d 746 (1986).

Stokes, A. P. (1975). *Church and State in the United States* (rev. ed.). Westport, Conn.: Greenwood Press.

Glossary

Appeal is the process whereby court decisions are examined by "higher" courts, that is, courts with more authority. Most decisions can be appealed at least once, although appellate courts sometimes can limit and choose the kind of cases they will hear.

Burden of Proof means that a party to a lawsuit has the obligation to present credible evidence to initiate or to satisfy his/her claim or defense of a claim. Often the burden of proof shifts from one party to the other as one party meets his/her burden. For example, if someone claiming clergy privileged communication meets his/her initial burden of proof that such a privilege should be enforced, it is then up to the other party to establish that the statutory criteria for privileged communications have not been met.

Civil law is the law of private rights, such as contracts, defamation (libel and slander), or torts. Punishments imposed for infractions of civil law are primarily monetary fines, as opposed to jail terms (see criminal law).

Common law is the body of law composed of court opinions and common practice.

Criminal law is the set of laws proscribing public wrongs committed against the state. These laws are enforced for the purpose of protecting the public health and safety. Enforcing agencies are government controlled, and the punishments can include both fines and incarceration.

A **defendant** is the party who defends against a suit. He/She may be sued civilly or be prosecuted by the state. The defendant is the second named party in the case name.

Felonies are a more serious class of criminal acts than misdemeanors. They may be punishable by fines *and* jail. Such jail terms normally exceed one year.

Heart balm statutes are state laws that abolish the right to bring suit for broken relationships or broken hearts, such as alienation of affections and a broken marriage promise.

Immunity means a privilege not to be sued, prosecuted, forced to testify in court, or forced to comply with some other legal requirement.

Informed consent indicates that any person giving his/her consent fully comprehends all the risks that the consent may entail. Informed consent must be a voluntary act.

Misdemeanor, as distinguished from felony, is a class of lesser criminal acts, usually punishable by fines or a jail term of less than one year.

Nonsuit means that the case ends without any ruling on the case's merits.

Overrule means to supersede a prior decision. A notable example of a court overruling a prior decision is when the Supreme Court superseded its (1896) decision of *Plessy v. Ferguson* with the landmark school desegregation decision in 1954 of *Brown v. Topeka Board of Education.*

Parens Patriae, literally "parent of the country," means a role played by authorities in place of parents or guardians. Such roles may be played by school authorities for their students.

Plaintiff means the party who initiates a civil case. In the case name, the plaintiff's name appears first and the defendant's name is listed second. On appeal, however, the plaintiff's name may appear second.

Precedent embodies previous case law upon which subsequent court decisions are based.

Privileged communication is an immunity (privilege) against testifying in court as to confidential information. Without the privilege, those who are called to testify must do so under the penalty of contempt of court (see subpoena).

When a case is **remanded,** the appellate court returns the case back to the trial court or the federal court returns the case to the state court for further action.

Stare decisis, "stable decisions," is a long-standing legal doctrine of maintaining consistency among judicial decisions. This consistency means that the court will use prior opinions (precedent) to guide its decision making.

Subpoena is a court order requiring court testimony. If a person is served with a subpoena, he/she is required to comply. It is a criminal violation (contempt of court) to refuse to comply with the subpoena.

Torts are part of the civil law that addresses harmful acts toward persons or property. "Torts" comes from a word meaning "twisted" (i.e., a tort is a "twisted" act). Tort law includes malpractice and professional negligence, personal injury cases (slip and fall), and automobile injuries, among other things.

LIST OF ABBREVIATIONS
USED IN REFERENCES*

A.2d Atlantic Reporter, second series. (In each citation where "2d" appears, the case reporter is in its second series.)

A.D. Appellate Division of the New York Supreme Court

aff'd Case has been affirmed on appeal.

BPC Business and Professional Code

Cal. California Reports, first series

Cal. 3d California Reports, third series

Cal. App. Reporter for the California Court of Appeals

Cal. App. 3d Reporter for the California Court of Appeals, third series

Cal. Rptr. California Reporter

Cert. denied Case was denied an appeal to the U.S. Supreme Court.

Cir. Circuit courts of the federal court system

Colo. Colorado Reports

---

*This list is not comprehensive. When a state abbreviation appears in citation parentheses, the abbreviation designates location. When a state abbreviation appears in a citation otherwise, the abbreviation designates a reporter system.

F.2d   Federal Reporter, second series (federal circuit court)

F. Supp.   Federal Supplement (federal district court)

Ga. App.   Georgia Court of Appeals

Ind.   Indiana Reports

Iowa   Iowa Reports

Kan. App.   Kansas Court of Appeals

Mass.   Reporter for the Massachusetts Supreme Judicial Court

M.D.N.C.   Middle District of North Carolina (the location of the federal district court)

Minn. App.   Minnesota Court of Appeals

Misc. 2d   New York Miscellaneous Reports, second series

Mo. App.   Missouri Court of Appeals

N.E.2d   North Eastern Reporter, second series

N.J. Super.   New Jersey Superior Court

N.W.2d   North Western Reporter, second series

N.Y.S.2d   West's New York Supplement Reporter, second series

Or.   Oregon Reports

Or. App.   Oregon Court of Appeals

P.2d   Pacific Reporter, second series

Pa. Super.   Pennsylvania Superior Court

rev'd.   Case was reversed.

S.C.   South Carolina Reporter

S. Ct.   Supreme Court Reporter

S.D.N.Y.   Southern District of the federal district court sitting in New York State

Serv.   Service

So.2d   Southern Reporter, second series

Supp.   Supplements to state codes

U.P.I.   (QuikNews) (computer database)

U.S.   United States Reporter of the Supreme Court

U.S.L.W.   United States Law Week Reporter

Vt.   Vermont Reports

Wash.   Washington (State) Reports

W.D. Mich.   Western District of the federal district court sitting in Michigan

West Supp.   Statutory supplement published by the West Publishing Company